GLOBALIZATION, GROWTH, AND POVERTY

A World Bank Policy Research Report

GLOBALIZATION, GROWTH, AND POVERTY

BUILDING AN INCLUSIVE WORLD ECONOMY

A copublication of the World Bank and
Oxford University Press

Oxford University Press ISBN 0-19-521608-3
World Bank ISBN 0-8213-5048-X

Cover photo credits
Front cover photos, courtesy of Guy Stubbs and the World Bank Photo Library.
Back cover photo, courtesy of Associated Press.

Library of Congress Cataloging-in-Publication Data has been applied for.

∞ *Text printed on paper that conforms to the American National Standard*
for Permanence of Paper for Printed Library Materials, Z39.48-1984

Contents

Maps

Tables

Foreword

GLOBALIZATION—THE GROWING INTEGRATION OF economies and societies around the world—is a complex process that affects many aspects of our lives. The terrorist attacks on the United States on September 11 were one aspect of globalization. Rapid growth and poverty reduction in China, India, and other countries that were poor 20 years ago is another. The development of the internet and easier communication and transportation around the world is a third. The spread of AIDS is part of globalization, as is the accelerated development of life-extending technologies. Something so complex cannot be analyzed in a single book, and our objective is more humble than examining all aspects of globalization. The focus of our research is the impact of economic integration on developing countries and especially on the poor people living in these countries. About one-fifth of the world's population lives on less than $1 per day, and that is unacceptable in a world of such plenty. Whether economic integration supports poverty reduction and how it can do so more effectively—these are the key questions that we ask.

Our research yields three main findings that bear on current policy debates about globalization. First, poor countries with around 3 billion people have broken into the global market for manufactures and services. Whereas 20 years ago most exports from developing countries were of primary commodities, now manufactures and services predominate. This successful *integration* has generally supported poverty reduction. Examples can be found among Chinese provinces, Indian states, and the countries of Bangladesh and Vietnam. The 'new globalizers' have experienced large-scale poverty reduction: during the 1990s the number of their people who were poor declined by 120 million. Integration would not have been feasible without a wide range of domestic reforms covering governance, the investment climate, and social service provision. But it also required international action, which provided access to foreign markets, technology, and aid.

The second finding concerns *inclusion* both across countries and within them. One of the most disturbing global trends of the past two decades is that countries with around 2 billion people are in danger of becoming marginal to the world economy. Incomes in these countries have been falling, poverty has been rising, and they participate less in trade today than they did 20 years ago. In the extreme, some of these are failed states, such as Afghanistan or the Democratic Republic of the Congo. The world has a large stake in helping countries integrate with the global economy, and we highlight a range of measures that would make this easier and lead to greater inclusion of countries in contemporary globalization. These measures range from better access to rich country markets to greater volumes of foreign aid, better managed.

Within countries that have succeeded in breaking into global manufacturing markets, integration has not, typically, led to greater income inequality. Nevertheless, there are both winners and losers from globalization. Both owners of firms and workers in protected sectors are likely to lose from liberalization and a more competitive economy, whereas consumers and those who find jobs in new firms will be among the winners. It is important to counter the risks of loss through social protection, and such measures are affordable in the context of the economic gains that the new globalizing countries are experiencing.

A third issue concerns *standardization* or *homogenization.* Opinion polls in diverse countries reveal an anxiety that economic integration will lead to cultural or institutional homogenization. Yet societies that are all fully integrated into the global economy differ enormously. Among the richest countries, Japan, Denmark, and the United States are each quite different in terms of culture, institutions, social policies, and inequality. Among the developing country globalizers, it is again striking that countries such as China, India, Malaysia, and Mexico have taken diverse routes toward integration and remain quite distinctive in terms of culture and institutions. Diversity may be more robust than is popularly imagined. Nevertheless, some recent developments in the global trading and investment regime are pushing countries toward an undesired standardization. It is important that global trade and investment agreements respect countries' freedoms in a range of areas from intellectual property rights, cultural goods, and environmental protection to social policies and labor standards. Globalization does not need homogenization, and it is important that diversity be respected in international agreements. There is also a real danger that the imposition of global standards could be used as the excuse for a resurgence of rich country protectionism.

In sum, global economic integration has supported poverty reduction and should not be reversed. But the world economy could be much more inclusive: the growth of global markets must not continue to bypass countries with 2 billion people. The rich countries can do much, both through aid and trade policies, to help the currently marginalized countries onto the path of integration that has already proved so effective for the new globalizers.

Nicholas Stern
Senior Vice President
and Chief Economist
The World Bank
December 2001

The Report Team

T HIS REPORT WAS PREPARED UNDER THE SUPERVISION OF Nicholas Stern, Chief Economist and Senior Vice President. It was written by Paul Collier (Director, Development Research Group) and David Dollar (Research Manager in the Development Research Group). The report draws on original research by these authors and by Ximena Clark, Richard Freeman, Mary Hallward-Driemeier, Christiane Kraus, Jean Lanjouw, Peter Lindert, Will Martin, Remco Oostendorp, Martin Rama, Sergio Schmukler, Zmarak Shalizi, John Sutton, Tony Venables, Jeff Williamson, Michael Woolcock, and Pablo Zoido-Lobaton. Their individual papers are available on our globalization website: www.worldbank.org/research/global. We thank for their excellent work Polly Means, who did the graphics; Emily Khine and Audrey Kitson-Walters, who processed the report; Andrew Phillips, who edited it; and Heather Worley and Susan Graham, who were in charge of production. We also thank for helpful comments on earlier drafts Caroline Anstey, Alan Gelb, Ian Goldin, Guillermo Perry, Guy Pfeffermann, Josef Ritzen, Halsey Rogers, and Roberto Zagha.

The judgments in this Policy Research Report do not necessarily reflect the views of the World Bank Board of Directors or the governments they represent.

Overview

SOCIETIES AND ECONOMIES AROUND THE WORLD ARE becoming more integrated. Integration is the result of reduced costs of transport, lower trade barriers, faster communication of ideas, rising capital flows, and intensifying pressure for migration. Integration—or "globalization"— has generated anxieties about rising inequality, shifting power, and cultural uniformity. This report assesses its impact and examines these anxieties. Global integration is already a powerful force for poverty reduction, but it could be even more effective. Some, but not all, of the anxieties are well-founded. Both global opportunities and global risks have outpaced global policy. We propose an agenda for action, both to enhance the potential of globalization to provide opportunities for poor people and to reduce and mitigate the risks it generates.

Globalization generally reduces poverty because more integrated economies tend to grow faster and this growth is usually widely diffused. As low-income countries break into global markets for manufactures and services, poor people can move from the vulnerability of grinding rural poverty to better jobs, often in towns or cities. In addition to this structural relocation, integration raises productivity job by job. Workers with the same skills—be they farmers, factory workers, or pharmacists— are less productive and earn less in developing economies than in advanced ones. Integration reduces these gaps. Rich countries maintain significant barriers against the products of poor countries, inhibiting this poverty-reducing integration. A "development round" of trade ne-gotiations could do much to help poor countries better integrate with the global economy and is part of our agenda for action.

Globalization also produces winners and losers, both between coun-tries and within them. Between countries, globalization is now mostly reducing inequality. About 3 billion people live in "new globalizing" developing countries. During the 1990s this group grew at 5 percent per capita compared to 2 percent for the rich countries. The number of extreme poor (living on less than $1 per day) in the new globalizers declined by 120 million between 1993 and 1998. However, many poor countries—with about 2 billion people—have been left out of the process of globalization. Many are becoming marginal to the world economy, often with declining incomes and rising poverty. Clearly, for this massive group of people, globalization is not working. Some of these countries have been handicapped by unfavorable geography, such as being landlocked and prone to disease. Others have been handicapped by weak policies, institutions, and governance; yet others by civil war. Addressing the marginalized areas is a key part of our agenda for action. Reducing poverty in these areas will require a combination of policy reform to create a better investment climate; development assistance to address problems of education and health; and out-migration to more favorable locations, both within and across national boundaries.

Within countries, globalization has not, on average, affected inequality, although behind the average there is much variation. The rapid growth in the new globalizers can be a political opportunity for redistribution policies that favor the poor, since higher-income groups need not lose absolutely. For example, programs specifically designed to promote non-farm employment can help people who remain in rural areas. There are also some predictable circumstances in which opening up is likely to increase inequality unless offset by other policies, such as when educational attainment is very unequal. Promoting education, particularly for poor people, is equalizing, improves health standards, and enhances the productivity growth that is the main engine of poverty reduction. The fact that globalization does not on average increase inequality within countries disguises the reality that there will be specific winners and losers in each society. Good social protection policies can be a key factor in helping people prosper in this more dynamic environment.

Finally, much of the concern about globalization involves issues of power, culture, and the environment. Globalization does involve shifts in power, but these do not always favor the already powerful. For example, China and India are rapidly becoming major economies; intensifying competition has forced corporations to reduce price mark-ups over cost; and many wages are rising rapidly in the new globalizers. Governments retain a wide range of choice, most notably in distributional policies. Due to globalization, policies to counter terrorism and civil war will need to be globally coordinated. Globalization poses cultural challenges: there is often greater diversity as foreign cultures and peoples are introduced. Sometimes foreign culture, or simply the sheer pace of economic change, threatens to displace local culture and societies can legitimately seek to protect it. Global growth also threatens the environment. Some pollution issues require local regulation. Governments may potentially compete to weaken regulations in a so-called race to the bottom. However, the evidence suggests that this is not happening: in key areas environmental standards are actually rising. Other issues, such as global warming, require a global response. That capacity has so far been lacking. But for the first time in history a global civil society has emerged—"globalization from below." This can become a powerful impetus to global collective action, both for improving the environment and for reducing poverty.

Globalization reduces poverty, but not everywhere

SINCE 1980 THERE HAS BEEN UNPRECEDENTED GLOBAL integration. In Chapter 1, we contrast this new wave of globalization with two previous waves. We analyze its processes and show how it is affecting poverty and equity.

The first wave of modern globalization took place from 1870 to 1914. Advances in transportation and negotiated reductions of barriers opened up the possibility for some countries to use their abundant land more productively. Flows of goods, capital, and labor all increased dramatically. Exports relative to world income nearly doubled to about 8 percent. Foreign capital more than tripled relative to income in the developing countries of Africa, Asia, and Latin America. Migration was even more dramatic. Sixty million people migrated from Europe, primarily its less developed parts, to North America and other parts of the New World. South-South labor flows were also substantial. The flows from densely populated China and India to less densely populated Sri Lanka, Burma, Thailand, the Philippines, and Vietnam were probably of the same order of magnitude as the movements from Europe to the Americas. The total labor flows during the first wave of globalization were nearly 10 percent of the world's population.

Global per capita income rose at an unprecedented rate, but not fast enough to prevent the number of poor people from rising. Among the globalizing countries there was convergence in income per capita, driven primarily by migration. However, there was a widening gap between the globalizers and those countries left behind, leading to increased world inequality.

A century ago globalization seemed as inevitable as it does today. However, incompetent economic policies, unemployment and nationalism drove governments into beggar-thy-neighbor protectionism. In retrospect, we can see the period encompassing the First World War, the Great Depression, and the Second World War as a giant step backward in global economic integration. By the late 1940s trade as a share of income was approximately back to its level of 1870: protectionism had erased 80 years of progress in transportation. During this period of inward-looking economic policies global growth slowed down: the growth of per capita income fell by around a third, and the number of poor people continued to rise. World inequality continued to increase; protectionism was clearly not equalizing. Despite the rise in poverty viewed in terms of income, this was a period of great advances in life expectancy due to the global spread of improvements in public health. This illustrates both that poverty is multidimensional and that not all its aspects are determined by economic performance.

The years from 1950 to 1980 saw a second wave of globalization, one that focused on integration among rich countries. Europe, North America, and Japan concentrated on restoring trade relations through a series of multilateral trade liberalizations under the auspices of the General Agreement on Tariffs and Trade (GATT). During this second wave most developing countries remained stuck in primary commodity exporting and were largely isolated from capital flows. In part this was due to their own inward-oriented policies. As a group the Organisation of Economic Co-operation and Development (OECD) economies surged ahead with unprecedented growth rates. There was convergence between them as integration proceeded: the industrial countries that were relatively poor grew fastest. Within most OECD countries there was a modest trend toward greater equality, aided by social welfare policies and programs. Growth in the developing countries also recovered, but less strongly, so the gap between rich and poor countries widened. The number of poor people continued to increase although there were continued gains in life expectancy. There was little net change in the distribution of income among and within developing countries.

The most recent wave of globalization—starting around 1980 and continuing today—has been spurred by technological advance in transport and communications technologies and by the choice of large developing countries to improve their investment climates and to open up to foreign trade and investment. For the first time, poor countries have been able to harness the potential of their abundant labor to break into global markets for manufactured goods and for services. Manufactures rose from less than a quarter of developing country exports in 1980 to more than 80 percent by 1998. Countries that strongly increased their participation in global trade and investment include Brazil, China, Hungary, India, and Mexico. Some 24 developing countries—with 3 billion people—have doubled their ratio of trade to income over the past two decades. The rest of the developing world actually trades less today than it did 20 years ago. The more globalized developing countries have increased their per capita growth rate from 1 percent in the 1960s, to 3 percent in the 1970s, 4 percent in the 1980s, and 5 percent in the 1990s. Their growth rates now substantially exceed those of the rich countries: they are catching up just as during earlier waves of globalization there was convergence among OECD countries (figure 1). While the new globalizers are beginning to catch up, much of the rest of the developing world—with about 2 billion people—is becoming marginalized. Their aggregate growth rate was actually negative in the 1990s.

The accelerated growth of recent globalizers is consistent with other cross-country statistical analyses that find that trade goes hand-in-hand with faster growth. The most that these studies can establish is that more trade is *correlated* with higher growth, and one must be careful about drawing conclusions on causality. Lindert and Williamson (2001b) suggest that: "The doubts that one can retain about each individual study threaten to block our view of the overall forest of evidence. Even though no one study can establish that openness to trade has unambiguously helped the representative Third World economy, the preponderance of evidence supports this conclusion" (pp. 29–30).

A widespread anxiety is that growing integration is leading to heightened inequalities within countries. Usually, this is not the case. Most of the globalizing developing countries have seen only small changes in household inequality, and inequality has declined in such countries as the Philippines and Malaysia. However, there are some important examples that go the other way. In Latin America, due to prior extreme inequalities in educational attainment, global integration has further widened wage inequalities. In China inequality has also risen, but the rise in Chinese inequality is far less problematic. Initially, China was both extremely equal and extremely poor. Domestic liberalization first unleashed rapid growth in rural areas. Since the mid-1980s there has also been rapid growth in urban agglomerations; this has increased inequality as the gap between rural and urban areas has widened. If this increase in inequality in China

Figure 1   Divergent paths of developing countries in the 1990s

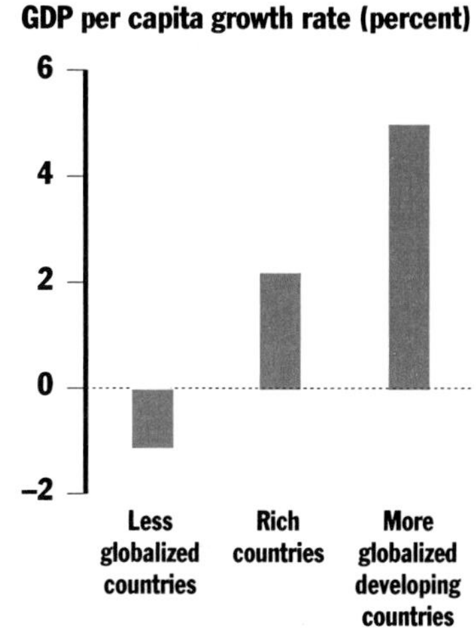

GDP per capita growth rate (percent)

Source: Dollar and Kraay (2001b).

5

has been the price of growth, it has paid off in terms of a massive reduction in poverty. The number of rural poor in the country declined from 250 million in 1978 to just 34 million in 1999.

The potential for global integration to reduce poverty is well illustrated by the cases of China, India, Uganda, and Vietnam. As Vietnam has integrated it has had a large increase in per capita income and no significant change in inequality. Thus, the income of the poor has risen dramatically and the level of absolute poverty has been cut in half in 10 years. Among the very poorest households, survey evidence shows that 98 percent became better off during the 1990s. This improved well-being is not just a matter of income. Child labor has declined and school enrollment has increased. Vietnam's exports directly provided income-earning opportunities for poor people: exports included labor-intensive products such as footwear and rice, which is produced by most low-income farmers.

India and Uganda also had rapid poverty reduction as they integrated with the global economy (figure 2). While some aspects of the data are controversial, the evidence for substantial poverty reduction in India in the 1990s is strong. In Uganda poverty fell by about 40 percent during the 1990s and school enrollments doubled. Globalization clearly can be a powerful force for poverty reduction.

About 2 billion people live in countries that are not participating strongly in globalization, many of them in Africa and the Former Soviet Union (FSU). Their exports are usually confined to a narrow range of primary

Figure 2   Poverty reduction in Uganda, India, Vietnam, and China closely related to growth

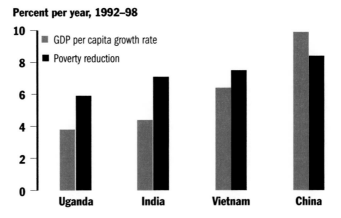

Percent per year, 1992–98

Note: India poverty reduction figure is for 1993–99.
Source: World Bank (2001d); Dollar (2001).

commodities. Such a concentration has made them highly prone to terms of trade shocks. There is also evidence that dependence upon primary commodity exports increases the risk of civil war. Hence, it is important for these countries to diversify their exports by breaking into global markets for manufactured goods and services where possible. Three schools of thought provide credible accounts of why this has not happened. One argues that countries have become marginalized as a result of poor policies and infrastructure, weak institutions, and corrupt governance. The implication is that integration requires not merely openness to trade and investment, but also complementary actions in a wide range of areas. A second school argues that the marginalized countries suffer from intrinsic disadvantages of adverse geography and climate. For example, landlocked countries may simply find it impossible to compete in the markets for global manufactures and services. One implication is that global programs are needed to assist these countries—for example, to counter malaria and to irrigate drought-prone agricultural areas. A third school combines the analysis of the first school with the conclusion of the second. It argues that as a result of a temporary phase of poor policies, some countries have permanently missed the opportunity to industrialize because agglomerations have been located elsewhere in the developing world. All three arguments are probably correct for parts of the marginalized world. However, policy does not have to decide among them. A successful and prudent strategy would combine opening up with the necessary complementary actions, while building the global coalitions needed to address the deep-seated structural problems that face many countries.

The striking divergence between the more globalized and less globalized developing countries since 1980 makes the aggregate performance of developing countries less meaningful. However, since 1980 the overall number of poor people has at last stopped increasing, and has indeed fallen by an estimated 200 million (figure 3). It is falling rapidly in the new globalizers and rising in the rest of the developing world. Non-income dimensions of poverty are also diverging. Life expectancy and schooling are rising in the new globalizers—to levels close to those prevailing in rich countries around 1960. They are falling in parts of Africa and the FSU.

Since 1980 world inequality has also stopped increasing, and may have started to fall. Participation in the world's industrial economy raises incomes, but for about a century only a minority of people participated and so global industrialization led to greater inequality. This third wave of globalization may mark the turning point at which participation has widened sufficiently for it to reduce both poverty and inequality.

Figure 3   World poverty, 1820–1998

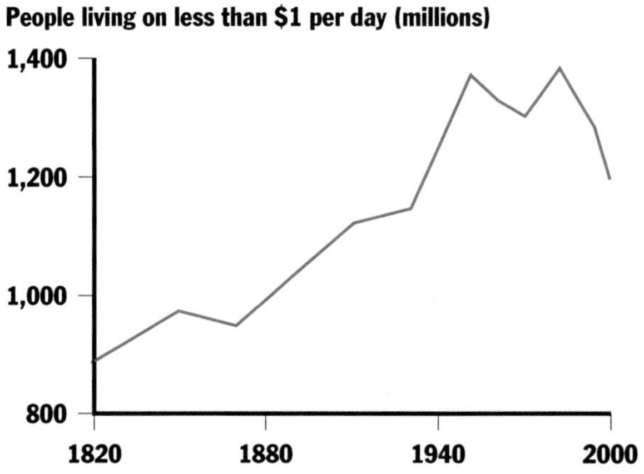

People living on less than $1 per day (millions)

Source: Bourguignon and Morrisson (2001); Chen and Ravallion (2001).

Improving the international architecture for integration

CHAPTER 2 FOCUSES ON THE GLOBAL AGENDA FOR TRADE policy, financial architecture, and migration. A distinctive feature of the current round of globalization is that many developing countries have cut their restrictions on imports in the past 20 years. The reduction in average tariffs is particularly striking in South Asia, from 65 percent in the early 1980s to about 30 percent today (figure 4). In Latin America and East Asia, average rates fell from 30 percent to about 10 percent. On average, liberalization efforts in Sub-Saharan Africa and in the Middle East and North Africa have been more limited, though there are individual countries such as Ethiopia and Uganda that have liberalized trade significantly and pursued other reforms. Most of these moves have been unilateral rather than under the auspices of multilateral negotiations through the GATT or it successor organization, the World Trade Organization (WTO). As countries such as China, India, and Mexico have opened up, their exports have shifted into manufactured products so that they are competing head-to-head with many of the products made in rich countries. In 1980 manufactured products comprised only 25 percent of developing country exports; by 1998 that figure had reached more than 80 percent.

While many developing countries have chosen to become more open economically, they continue to confront protectionism in the rich

Figure 4   Average unweighted tariff rates by region

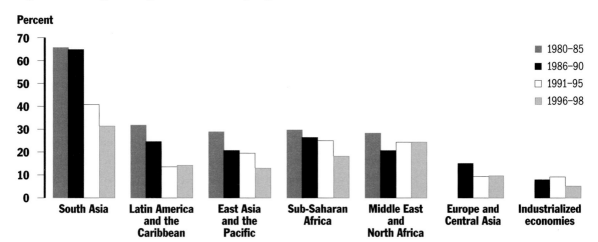

Percent

Legend:
- 1980–85
- 1986–90
- 1991–95
- 1996–98

Regions: South Asia | Latin America and the Caribbean | East Asia and the Pacific | Sub-Saharan Africa | Middle East and North Africa | Europe and Central Asia | Industrialized economies

Source: World Bank (2001c).

countries. Average tariff rates in rich countries are low, but they maintain barriers in exactly the areas where developing countries have comparative advantage: agriculture and labor-intensive manufactures. Protection in rich countries costs developing countries more than $100 billion per year, twice the total volume of aid from North to South. Barriers in developing countries are three times higher than in OECD countries. Given that developing countries now trade much more with each other than in the past, and 70 percent of the tariff barriers on developing country exports come from other developing countries, there would be significant gains from another round of multilateral trade liberalization within the framework of the WTO.

A "development round" of trade liberalization should focus on improving market access of developing countries to rich country markets and to each other's markets. However, such a "development round" is threatened by narrow protectionist interests in the North. Protectionists are seeking to load up the trade agenda with a host of other, institutional development issues. If the rich countries insist on institutional harmonization in areas such as intellectual property rights and standards for health, labor, and the environment as a prerequisite for market access, then prospects for greater trade between North and South will be greatly diminished. This report argues that many developing countries *are* strengthening labor conditions and environmental policies and that there is much more that the world can do in support. The threat of trade sanctions through the WTO is not supportive but destructive. What is needed is greater support for *domestic* actions to improve labor and environmental outcomes.

Hand-in-hand with trade liberalization, developing countries have reduced restrictions on foreign investment. Private capital flows to developing countries—especially foreign direct investment (FDI)—have soared. These flows bring benefits: increased supply of capital and access to technology, management, and markets. While private flows to the new globalizers have risen dramatically, the less globalized countries have often experienced capital flight—by 1990 about 40 percent of Africa's private wealth was held outside the continent. Further, official development assistance from rich countries to poor ones has declined. For the poor locations that do not now benefit greatly from globalization, there is a need for more aid, better managed.

While there are large and clear benefits from reducing trade barriers, exposure to world capital markets carries both benefits and considerable risks. Countries need good institutions and policies for strong and sustained benefits from financial integration. Without a sound domestic financial system, integration with global capital markets can lead to disastrous results, as it did in Thailand, Indonesia, and the Republic of Korea in 1997. Foreign investment in financial and accounting services can help with the needed strengthening. Even with the best of institutions and policies, countries can be buffeted by international financial crises because these markets are subject to irrational boom and bust cycles. Better international coordination is needed on accounting standards and transparency and on the management of incipient financial crises in such a way that adequate liquidity is ensured for countries with sound policies while at the same time private investors are discouraged from and penalized for risky lending practices.

Migration is the third main global flow. The role of migration is connected to the importance of geography. In regions with poor institutions and high transport costs wages will be low, and free movement of goods and capital will not bring those wages into line with wages in good locations. Further, within good locations there will be clustering as long as agglomeration economies are important, and hence wage pressure to migrate to towns and cities.

We noted above that during the first great wave of globalization about 10 percent of the world's population moved permanently to a new country. Even greater numbers migrated from rural areas to cities within countries. The same forces operate today. A study following individual, legal migrants from Mexico to the United States found that on average they left jobs at home paying \$31 per week and on arrival in the United States could immediately earn \$278 per week (a nine-fold increase). Similarly, Indonesian workers earn 28 cents per day at home, compared to \$2 or more in next-door Malaysia. Clearly there are huge real gains to individual workers who migrate to more developed economies.

While economic pressures for migration are strong, legal migration is highly restricted. Compared to 100 years ago, the world is much less globalized when it comes to labor flows. The total number of migrants living in countries not of their citizenship is only about 2 percent of the world's population. At the same time, pressures for migration are mounting. The labor force in OECD countries is aging, while the labor force in the developing world is surging because of high birth rates. Each year 83 million people are added to world population, 82 million of them in developing countries. In Japan and the European Union (EU), the ratio of workers to retirees will decline from five to one today to three to one in 2015, without greater migration. That will put a strain on social security systems.

Potentially, there is mutual economic benefit in combining the capital and technology of the OECD countries with the labor of the developing world. To some extent that can occur through the flow of capital and production to developing countries. But geographic factors make it unlikely that capital flows and trade will eliminate the economic rationale for migration. Too many parts of the developing world have poor institutions and infrastructure that will not attract production; at the same time, some of the existing production networks in the North are too deeply rooted to move. Institutional and policy reform and infrastructure investments in lagging developing countries could address the first concern and reduce, though not eliminate, economic pressures for migration.

The experiences of Mexico and the United States illustrate how migration can be a positive factor for both economies. About 7 million Mexican citizens are living legally in the United States, along with an estimated additional 3 million undocumented Mexican workers. This represents about 10 percent of Mexico's population and an even larger share of the Mexican labor force. Their work in the United States takes pressure off the Mexican labor market (raising wages there) and leads to a significant flow of remittances to relatives back home. In the United States, this labor inflow was a key factor contributing to sustained growth with low inflation in the 1990s. However, migration into the United States is estimated to have reduced the relative wage of unskilled workers by 5 percent, once again demonstrating that globalization typically produces winners and losers.

OECD countries are in general highly restrictive about migration, and they tend to discriminate in favor of educated workers (leading to a so-called "brain drain" from developing countries). Labor flows would make a greater contribution to poverty reduction if immigration policies were more neutral and allowed more unskilled workers to immigrate.

Strengthening domestic institutions and policies

INTEGRATION IS NOT PRIMARILY THE RESULT OF TRADE policy. It is also affected by a host of other institutions and policies. Chapter 3 focuses on this agenda. Countries such as China, India, and Mexico have taken different approaches to integration. There are common issues that must be addressed, but different institutional arrangements and policies for tackling them. Two of the important issues that need to be faced are the investment climate and social protection for workers.

Firms in open economies face more competition. Competition brings many good effects, but there is more entry and exit of firms—"churning"—than in relatively closed economies. Studies of Chile, Colombia, and Morocco after liberalization found that one-quarter to one-third of manufacturing firms turned over in a typical four-year period. Recent evidence from surveys of firms shows that it is unusual for manufacturing plants to shift from domestic production to exporting. For example, three-quarters of exporting plants in Morocco had exported from their first year of operation. Thus, the process of integrating into world markets is likely to require the opening of new plants and the closure of others.

Chapter 3 highlights other stylized facts about domestic firms in open economies. First, while production often becomes more concentrated (leading to fewer firms), the presence of imports leads to a more competitive market and lower price-cost mark-ups. Second, there is some evidence of technology spillovers from foreign trade and investment raising the productivity of domestic firms. Third, there can be learning and threshold effects of exporting that create a better environment for productivity growth of domestic firms.

Individual cases and firm-level studies reveal that developing country firms can be competitive. However, they are often hampered by a poor investment climate—including inefficient regulation, corruption, infrastructure weaknesses, and poor financial services. A recent study of India concludes that it is possible to measure the quality of the investment climate through firm surveys and that this climate is important. With the same trade and macro policies (which are national level), Indian states are getting widely different results from liberalization. "Good climate" states have more efficient regulation and better infrastructure (the typical small enterprise is using the Internet to do business), while "poor climate" states lag behind. Not surprisingly, the states with good climates are getting both more domestic and more foreign investment.

Thus, locations within the developing world that are benefiting strongly from globalization have created a reasonably good investment climate in which firms can start up and prosper (and exit if they are not successful). Coastal China and northern Mexico are other examples, and here too poverty reduction is quite strong.

Small and medium-sized firms suffer from a poor investment climate even more than the bigger firms. Further, we should emphasize that a good investment climate is crucial for the development of rural as well as urban areas. Off-farm employment is a crucial element in raising rural incomes, and farming suffers just as much from a weak investment climate as other productive activities.

Many of the regions that did not participate strongly in the global economy in the 1990s had problems with property rights and overall investment climate. Burma, Nigeria, Pakistan, the Russian Federation, and the Indian state of Uttar Pradesh are examples. These locations could use the international market for services (such as banking, telecommunications, and power) to improve their investment climates. The successful locations have devised their own solutions. China, India, and Mexico have all taken different approaches to opening up, suited to their own circumstances. This diversity of experience among successful globalizers is one reason why any efforts to promote institutional harmonization should take careful account of differing circumstances. They should not be linked to trade agreements in any mechanical or formulaic way.

Together with greater "churning" of firms comes higher labor market turnover, which can be one of the most disruptive aspects of global economic integration. In the long run workers gain from integration. Wages have grown twice as fast in the more globalized developing countries than in the less globalized ones, and faster than in rich countries as well (figure 5). The short-run effects, however, can be quite different. There

Figure 5   Wage growth by country group

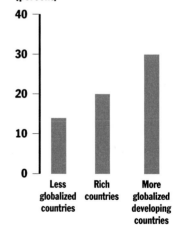

Growth between 1980s and 1990s (percent)

Source: Freeman, Oostendorp, and Rama (2001).

is evidence that the wages of formal sector workers are reduced by trade openness and increased by direct foreign investment. Thus, in an economy that liberalizes trade and gets little foreign investment (either because the investment climate is weak or simply because there is a lagged response of investors), opening up can lead to temporary declines in formal sector wages.

There is also evidence that openness—especially to FDI—increases the return to education and raises the skill premium (the extra pay that skilled workers get relative to unskilled workers). Case studies of transition economies and Latin America have found that skill premiums increase after liberalization. Trade liberalization in Costa Rica led to higher demand and higher wages for more skilled workers. After liberalization in Brazil there was a higher return to workers with a college education and a decreased return to those with intermediate levels of education. These findings highlight the importance of complementary policies both for social protection (to help with temporary unemployment) and for education. An increased skill premium can be a good thing because it encourages more investment in education. However, if the education system is not serving all levels of society well, then wages could become even more unequal.

Some of the important losers from globalization will be formal sector workers in protected industries. The adjustment is likely to be especially tough for older workers. Government social protection and labor market policies are very important—both for the immediate welfare of affected workers and for the longer-term welfare of all workers. To get reforms underway may require one-time compensation schemes for workers who would otherwise suffer large losses. Well-designed unemployment insurance and severance pay systems can provide protection to formal sector workers in an environment that will now have more entry and exit of firms. The poorest people cannot be reached by such systems, but there is huge potential to reduce their vulnerability to shocks through self-targeting programs such as food-for-work schemes. Social protection can be a dynamic force for growth and innovation beyond the gaining of acceptance for change—it can be crucial to the ability of poor people to take the risks involved in entrepreneurship. Finally, the combination of openness and a well-educated labor force produces especially good results for poverty reduction and human welfare. Hence, a good education system that provides opportunities for all is critical for success in this globalizing world.

Power, culture, and the environment

S O FAR, WE HAVE FOCUSED ON INCOME, INCOME DISTRIBUTION, and poverty. But much of the anxiety surrounding globalization concerns issues of power, culture, and the environment. Chapter 4 discusses these concerns.

A recent poll of 20,000 people in 20 countries found that by a margin of two to one people thought globalization would materially benefit their families (Environics 2001). (The survey included developing countries such as Brazil, China, India, and Nigeria.) But while people expect the kind of material benefits that we have documented in our report, they also express serious concerns and even fears. More than half of those polled were convinced that globalization threatens their country's unique culture. Citizens also perceive a lack of global governance in important areas. About four in 10 respondents named human rights as the area most in need of stronger international control, while three in 10 said that global environmental action was the highest priority. One in 10 thought that international action on workers' rights was a priority.

The United States is the largest and in some respects the most successful economy on earth, giving millions of poor people, many of them immigrants from developing countries, an opportunity to rise to prosperity. But it is not the only model of success. Several economies match or exceed the American level of income per capita while having radically different policies and more equal social outcomes. For example, Austria, Belgium, Denmark, Japan, and Norway are open economies. All have far less inequality than the United States with similar average income. By combining prosperity with equity they are the closest the world has yet come to eradicating poverty. Voters in the United States and these five countries have chosen substantially different models, all of which work given their respective histories. Not only is there no ultimate model of success, there is no fixed formula for reaching success. China, India, and Mexico all globalized during the 1990s as a result of far-reaching reform programs, but the content of these programs has differed.

Culturally, as societies integrate, in many respects they become more diverse: Ikea has brought Swedish design to Russians, co-existing with Russian design; Indian immigrants and McDonald's have brought chicken tikka and hamburgers to Britain, co-existing with fish and chips. However, without policies to foster local and other cultural traditions, globalization may indeed lead to a dominance of American culture.

In most developing countries the state is smaller relative to national income than in either the United States or the five high-income, high-equity countries noted above. Successful globalization—on any of these models—usually *enlarges* the state, both absolutely and relatively. However, globalization weakens some aspects of government, making some policy instruments ineffective.

Globalization will usually *weaken* monopolies. As countries open their markets, national monopoly producers face competition from foreign firms. However, one firm will occasionally get a sufficiently large global technological advantage that it acquires a temporary global monopoly, and more commonly oligopolies exert global market power. Such cases pose severe challenges to national anti-trust regulators. Further, there are charges that in developing countries some foreign firms may lobby or bribe to gain special privileges, for example, in telecommunications or minerals.

As global trade becomes more firmly based upon a legal framework, this potentially enhances the power of the developing countries: the weak need rules more than the strong. However, there is a danger that the rules come to favor the strong. For example, rich and poor countries have somewhat different interests regarding intellectual property and global warming. Developing countries want to keep some knowledge as a public good, while industrial countries prefer to turn it into a private good in order to reward innovation. Developing countries will suffer most from global warming, while rich countries are generating most of the carbon dioxide (CO_2) that is causing the problem. In bargaining to achieve fair rules on such issues, poor countries are handicapped by both their poverty and their fragmentation.

Globalization does not have to undermine national and local environmental standards through a so-called race to the bottom. Despite widespread fears, there is no evidence of a decline in environmental standards. In fact, a recent study of air quality in major industrial centers of the new globalizers found that it had improved significantly in all of them. A positive side of globalization is that communities can learn from each other about successful strategies to control pollution. Developing countries usually have serious problems enforcing regulations in the face of powerful vested interests. Indonesia improved compliance dramatically through a program in which environmentally dangerous factories were publicly identified, leading communities to organize against these polluters. Other communities have learned from this example and are introducing similar programs.

As with core labor standards, some groups in the rich countries are proposing that environmental regulations be policed through WTO sanctions. There are better ways to empower local communities. WTO sanctions would carry the risk of being hijacked by protectionist lobbies in rich countries and end up by restricting the opportunities of poor ones.

Some environmental issues, such as global warming, are intrinsically global. They require international cooperation, and the habit of such cooperation is easier in an integrated world. There is broad agreement among scientists that human activity has led to global warming and that much greater climate change is in store unless collective, corrective actions are taken. Where the problem comes from is clear. Seven economies (the so-called E-7) account for 70 percent of CO_2 emissions. The United States, with only 4 percent of the world's population, emits nearly 25 percent of greenhouse gases. China is the second largest emitter, followed by the EU, the Russian Federation, Japan, India, and Brazil. In per capita terms, the United States (with 20 metric tons per capita) is far ahead of other economies in terms of CO_2 emissions (figure 6).

It is important for the world that the major emitting countries agree on a way to reduce greenhouse gases. This is a classic collective action problem in which each country is reluctant to move on its own because much of the benefit of its reduction in greenhouse gases will accrue to others. The Kyoto protocol is an important step forward in collaborative action to address global warming.

Figure 6 Per capita CO_2 emissions in the E-7 economies, 1998

Annual emissions (metric tons)

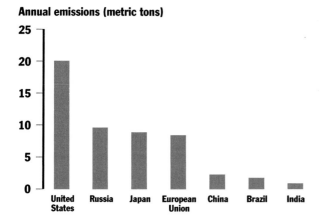

Source: Kraus and Shalizi (2001).

An agenda for action

RECENT GLOBALIZATION HAS BEEN A FORCE FOR POVERTY reduction, and has helped some large poor countries to narrow the gap with rich countries. However, some of the widespread anxieties are well founded: globalization could be much more effective for poor people, and its adverse effects could be substantially reduced. In important respects global policies are not keeping pace with global opportunities and global risks. In our report we propose an agenda for action, both global and local, that could make globalization work better and help countries and people that have been marginalized. In part our agenda overlaps with the agenda of those who protest globalization, but it is diametrically opposed to the nationalism, protectionism, and anti-industrial romanticism that is all too prominent. Our study highlights many actions that could help make globalization more beneficial. Of these, we will emphasize seven that we see as particularly important for making globalization work for the poor.

Participation in an expanding global market has basically been a positive force for growth and poverty reduction in developing countries, which is why so many countries have chosen to become more open to foreign trade and investment. Very significant barriers to trade still remain, however, and a *first* area for action is a "development round" of trade negotiations. A "development round" should focus first and foremost on market access. Rich countries maintain protections in exactly the areas where developing countries have comparative advantage, and there would be large gains to poor countries if these were reduced. Furthermore, developing countries would gain a lot from better access to each other's markets—barriers between them are still higher than those from developed countries. These improvements in access are best negotiated in a multilateral context.

Developing countries have a good argument that trade agreements should not impose labor or environmental standards on poor countries. Communities all over the world are struggling to improve living standards and labor and environmental conditions. There are positive ways that rich countries can support this. A real and positive commitment, however, requires real resources (more below on this). Imposing trade sanctions on countries that do not meet first-world standards for labor and environmental conditions can have deeply damaging effects on the living standards of poor people and for that reason is unconstructive. Furthermore, there is all too much danger that trade sanctions to enforce these standards will become new forms of protectionism that make the poor worse off. The more general point here is that trade agreements should leave countries free to take different institutional approaches to environmental standards, social protection, cultural preservation, and other issues. Among globalized countries there is great diversity of institutions and cultures, and we see no reason why economic integration cannot respect that.

Our research shows that open trade and investment policies are not going to do much for poor countries if other policies are bad. The locations in the developing world that are prospering during this most recent wave of globalization are ones that have created reasonably good investment climates in which firms, particularly small domestic firms, can start up, prosper, and expand. Hence, a *second* key area for action is improving the investment climate in developing countries. A sound investment climate is not one full of tax breaks and subsidies for firms. It is rather an environment of good economic governance—control of corruption, well-functioning bureaucracies and regulation, contract enforcement, and protection of property rights. Connectivity to other markets within a country and globally (through transport and telecommunications infrastructure) is a key part of a good investment climate. A bad investment climate hits agriculture and small firms even harder than bigger firms.

Developing a sound investment climate is primarily a national and local responsibility and should focus particularly on the problems facing small firms. Employment in the small and medium-sized firms in towns and rural areas will be central to raising the living standards of the rural poor. Communities can use foreign investment and the international market for services to strengthen the investment climate. The presence of foreign banks in the local market strengthens the financial infrastructure. With the right incentives, foreign investment can efficiently provide power, ports, telecommunications, and other business services.

The evidence is quite strong that integration with the global market raises the return to education in different types of countries (both rich and poor). The higher return to education can be a positive thing, as it encourages households to invest in their children. But this highlights the importance of good delivery of education and health services—the *third* element in our agenda. If poor people have little or no access to health and education services then it is very hard for them to benefit from the growth spurred by integration. With poor social services, globalization can easily lead to mounting inequality within a country and persistence of extreme poverty. For the newly globalizing developing countries as a group, there has been impressive progress in educational attainment—especially for primary education—and decline in infant mortality, suggesting that many locations have made the complementary investments in social services that are critical to ensure that the poor benefit from growth. The combination of strong education for poor people and a more positive investment climate is critical for empowering poor people to participate in the benefits of a more strongly expanding economy. But empowerment goes much deeper than this. It is about organizing property rights and governance in a way that involves poor people in decisions that affect their lives.

While integration has on average been a positive force for growth and poverty reduction in developing countries, there are inevitably specific winners and losers, especially in the short run. This is true in rich and poor countries. The firm-level evidence shows that much of the dynamic benefit of open trade and investment comes from more "churning" of plants—less efficient ones die, and new ones start up and expand. With this comes more labor market churning as well—probably the key reason why globalization is so controversial. It raises wages on average in both rich and poor countries, but there are some significant losers. Thus, the *fourth* area for action is to provide social protection tailored to the more dynamic labor market in an open economy. This is important to help individual workers who will lose in the short run from opening up, as well as to create a solid social foundation on which households—especially poor ones—feel comfortable taking risks and showing entrepreneurship. We try to document what works in a relatively rich country, and for formal sector workers, and what works in poor countries and for the large number of poor in the informal sector and rural areas. If policymakers do not put workable social protection measures into place, then many individual people will be hurt and the whole integration undertaking becomes suspect.

The *fifth* component of our action program is a greater volume of foreign aid, better managed. Aid should be targeted to a number of different problems. The evidence shows that, when low-income countries reform and improve the investment climate and social services, private investment—both domestic and foreign—responds with a lag. It is precisely in this environment that large-scale aid can have a great impact on growth and poverty reduction. Thus, while creating a sound policy environment is primarily a national and local responsibility, the world can help societies making difficult changes with financial support. Supporting low-income reformers—both at the national level and at the local level—is a key role for aid. Another important role for aid is to address some of the specific health and geographic challenges of marginalized countries and people. We have emphasized that there are locations that face difficult geographic challenges and that policy reform alone is not going to do much in these places. More aid should be targeted to research into health and agricultural technologies that could make a large difference in locations suffering from malaria and other challenges. Beyond research, there is obviously a need for assistance to deliver these health innovations to those who would benefit from them.

Our *sixth* area for action is debt relief. This is a kind of aid, but we do not want our recommendation here to get lost in our more general call for greater aid. Many of the marginalized countries, especially in Africa, are burdened with unsustainable debts. Reducing the debt burdens of these countries will be one factor enabling them to participate more strongly in globalization. Debt relief is particularly powerful when combined with policy reform (improvements in the investment climate and social services). Debt relief should make a significant difference for countries that have reasonably sound policy environments for poverty reduction, as in the Heavily Indebted Poor Country (HIPC) initiative. It is important to put debt relief in the larger context of the overall foreign aid for marginalized countries. Debt relief should not come out of the existing envelope for aid (in which case little of real value will result) but rather needs to be complemented with greater overall volumes of assistance.

The six areas that we have highlighted for policy action on globalization are primarily in the economic realm and aim to raise the income and living standards of poor people. However, our report also examines a wide range of non-economic issues—power, culture, environment—and presents evidence about the effect of globalization on these important issues. We highlight many specific actions that can mitigate the risks and costs of globalization. Here in the action program, the *seventh* measure to highlight is the importance of tackling greenhouse gases and global warming. There is broad agreement among scientists that human activity is leading to climate change and that disastrous global warming is in store unless collective, corrective action is taken. This is one example of a critical area in which there a lack of effective global cooperation at this point. It is also one of the global problems that is going to particularly burden poor countries and poor people if it is not addressed.

The falling costs of communications, information, and transport that have contributed to globalization will not be reversed, but the reduction in trade and investment barriers could be reversed by protectionism and nationalism—as happened in the 1930s. However, protectionism and nationalism would be a profoundly damaging reaction to the challenges created by globalization. The problems must be addressed, but they are manageable. The reasonable concerns about globalization can be met without sacrificing the potential for global economic integration to dramatically benefit poor countries and poor people. Many poor people are benefiting from globalization. The challenge is to bring more of them into this process, not to retreat to the insularity and nationalism of the 1930s.

CHAPTER ONE

The New Wave of Globalization and Its Economic Effects

S INCE ABOUT 1980 THERE HAS BEEN UNPRECEDENTED global economic integration. Globalization has happened before, but not like this. Economic integration occurs through trade, migration, and capital flows. Figure 1.1 tracks these flows. World trade is measured relative to world income. Capital flows are proxied by the stock of foreign capital in developing countries relative to their GDP. Migration is proxied by the number of immigrants to the United States. Historically, before about 1870 none of these flows was sufficiently large to warrant the term globalization.

Figure 1.1   Three waves of globalization

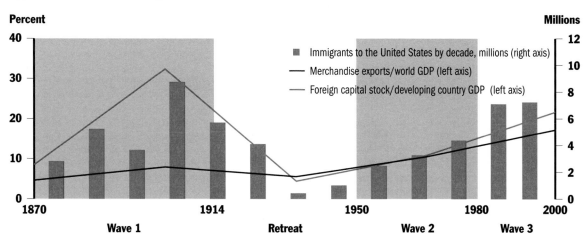

Source: Foreign capital stock/developing country GDP: Maddison (2001), table 3.3; Merchandise exports/world GDP: Maddison (2001), table F-5; Migration: Immigration and Naturalization Service (1998).

For about 45 years, starting around 1870, all these flows rapidly became substantial, driven by falling transport costs. What had been many separate national economies started to integrate: the world's economies globalized. However, globalization is not an inevitable process; this first wave was reversed by a retreat into nationalism. Between 1914 and 1945 transport costs continued to fall, but trade barriers rose as countries followed beggar-thy-neighbor policies. By the end of that period trade had collapsed back to around its 1870 level. After 1945 governments cooperated to rein in protectionism. As trade barriers came down, and transport costs continued to fall, trade revived. This second wave of globalization, which lasted until around 1980, was approximately a return to the patterns of the first wave.

Since 1980 many developing countries—the "new globalizers"— have broken into world markets for manufactured goods and services. There has been a dramatic rise in the share of manufactures in the exports of developing countries: from about 25 percent in 1980 to more than 80 percent today. There has also been a substantial increase in FDI. This marks an important change: low-income countries are now competing head-on with high-income countries while previously they specialized in primary commodities. During this new wave of global market integration, world trade has grown massively. Markets for merchandise are now much more integrated than ever before.

In this chapter we contrast this new third wave of globalization with the two previous waves. We analyze its main processes and show how it is affecting poverty and inequality.

Previous waves of globalization and reversals

MOST DEVELOPING COUNTRIES HAVE TWO POTENTIAL sources of comparative advantage in international markets: abundant labor and abundant land. Before about 1870 neither of these potentials was realized and international trade was negligible.

The first wave of globalization: 1870–1914

The first wave of global integration, from 1870 to 1914, was triggered by a combination of falling transport costs, such as the switch from sail to steamships, and reductions in tariff barriers, pioneered by an

Anglo-French agreement. Cheaper transport and the lifting of man-made barriers opened up the possibility of using abundant land. New technologies such as railways created huge opportunities for land-intensive commodity exports. The resulting pattern of trade was that land-intensive primary commodities were exchanged for manufactures. Exports as a share of world income nearly doubled to about 8 percent (Maddison 2001).

The production of primary commodities required people. Sixty million migrated from Europe to North America and Australia to work on newly available land. Because land was abundant in the newly settled areas, incomes were high and fairly equal, while the labor exodus from Europe tightened labor markets and raised wages both absolutely and relative to the returns on land. South-South labor flows were also extensive (though less well documented). Lindert and Williamson (2001b) speculate that the flows from densely populated China and India to less densely populated Sri Lanka, Burma, Thailand, the Philippines, and Vietnam were of the same order of magnitude as the movements from Europe to the Americas.[1] That would make the total labor flows during the first wave of globalization nearly 10 percent of the world's population.

The production of primary commodities for export required not just labor but large amounts of capital. As of 1870 the foreign capital stock in developing countries was only about 9 percent of their income (figure 1.1). However, institutions needed for financial markets were copied. These institutions, combined with the improvements in information permitted by the telegraph, enabled governments in developing countries to tap into the major capital markets. Indeed, during this period around half of all British savings were channeled abroad. By 1914 the foreign capital stock of developing countries had risen to 32 percent of their income.

Globally, growth accelerated sharply. Per capita incomes, which had risen by 0.5 percent per year in the previous 50 years, rose by an annual average of 1.3 percent. Did this lead to more or less equality? The countries that participated in it often took off economically, both the exporters of manufactures, people and capital, and the importers. Argentina, Australia, New Zealand, and the United States became among the richest countries in the world by exporting primary commodities while importing people, institutions, and capital. All these countries left the rest of the world behind.

Between the globalizing countries themselves there was convergence. Mass migration was a major force equalizing incomes between them. "Emigration is estimated to have raised Irish wages by 32 percent, Italian by 28 percent and Norwegian by 10 percent. Immigration is estimated to have lowered Argentine wages by 22 percent, Australian by 15 percent, Canadian by 16 percent and American by 8 percent." Indeed, migration was probably more important than either trade or capital movements (Lindert and Williamson 2001b).

The impact of globalization on inequality *within* countries depended in part on the ownership of land. Exports from developing countries were land-intensive primary commodities. Within developing countries this benefited predominantly the people who owned the land. Since most were colonies, land ownership itself was subject to the power imbalance inherent in the colonial relationship. Where land ownership was concentrated, as in Latin America, increased trade could be associated with increased inequality. Where land was more equally owned, as in West Africa, the benefits of trade were spread more widely. Conversely, in Europe, the region importing land-intensive goods, globalization ruined landowners. For example, Cannadine (1990) describes the spectacular economic collapse of the English aristocracy between 1880 and 1914. In Europe the first wave of globalization also coincided with the establishment for the first time in history of the great legislative pillars of social protection—free mass education, worker insurance, and pensions (Gray 1998).

Ever since 1820—50 years before globalization—world income inequality as measured by the mean log deviation had started to increase drastically (figure 1.2).[2] This continued during the first wave of globalization. Despite widening world inequality, the unprecedented increase in growth reduced poverty as never before. In the 50 years before 1870, the incidence of poverty had been virtually constant, falling at the rate of just 0.3 percent per year. During the first globalization wave, the rate of decline more than doubled to 0.8 percent. Even this was insufficient to offset the increase in population growth, so that the absolute number of poor people increased.

The retreat into nationalism: 1914–45

Technology continued to reduce transport costs: during the inter-war years sea freight costs fell by a third. However, trade policy went into reverse.

As Mundell (2000) puts it: "The twentieth century began with a highly efficient international monetary system that was destroyed in World War I,

Figure 1.2   Worldwide household inequality, 1820–1910

Mean log deviation

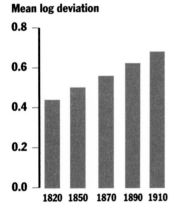

Source: Bourguignon and Morrisson (2001).

and its bungled recreation in the inter-war period brought on the great depression." In turn, governments responded to depression by protectionism: a vain attempt to divert demand into their domestic markets. The United States led the way into the abyss: the Smoot-Hawley tariff, which led to retaliation abroad, was the first: between 1929 and 1933 U.S. imports fell by 30 percent and, significantly, exports fell even more, by almost 40 percent.

Globally, rising protectionism drove international trade back down. By 1950 exports as a share of world income were down to around 5 percent—roughly back to where it had been in 1870. Protectionism had undone 80 years of technical progress in transport.

During the retreat into nationalism capital markets fared even worse than merchandise markets. Most high-income countries imposed controls preventing the export of capital, and many developing countries defaulted on their liabilities. By 1950 the foreign capital stock of developing countries was reduced to just 4 percent of income—far below even the modest level of 1870.

Unsurprisingly, the retreat into nationalism produced anti-immigrant sentiment and governments imposed drastic restrictions on newcomers. For example, immigration to the United States declined from 15 million during 1870–1914 to 6 million between 1914 and 1950.

The massive retreat from globalization did not reverse the trend to greater world inequality. By 1950 the world was far less equal than it had been in 1914 (figure 1.3). Average incomes were, however, substantially lower than had the previous trend been maintained: the world rate of growth fell by about a third. The world's experiment with reversing globalization showed that it was entirely possible but not attractive. The economic historian Angus Maddison summarizes it thus: "Between 1913 and 1950 the world economy grew much more slowly than in 1870–1913, world trade grew much less than world income, and the degree of inequality between regions increased substantially" (Maddison 2001, p. 22).

The combination of a slowdown in growth and a continued increase in inequality sharply reduced the decline in the incidence of poverty—approximately back to what it had been in the period from 1820 to 1870. The decline in the incidence was now well below the rate of population growth, so that the absolute number of poor people increased by about 25 percent. Despite the rise in poverty viewed in terms of income, this was the great period of advances in life expectancy, due to the global

Figure 1.3 Worldwide household inequality, 1910–50

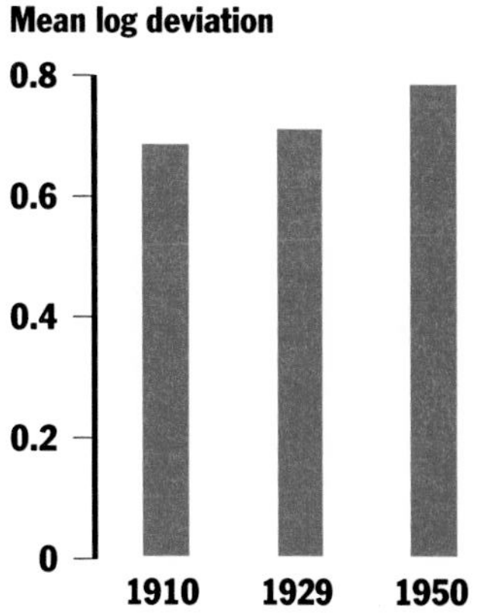

Source: Bourguignon and Morrisson (2001).

spread of improvements in public health. Poverty is multi-dimensional, and not all its aspects are determined by economic performance.

The second wave of globalization: 1945–80

The horrors of the retreat into nationalism gave an impetus to internationalism. The same sentiments that led to the founding of the United Nations persuaded governments to cooperate to reduce the trade barriers they had previously erected. However, trade liberalization was selective both in terms of which countries participated and which products were included. Broadly, by 1980 trade between developed countries in manufactured goods had been substantially freed of barriers, but barriers facing developing countries had been substantially removed only for those primary commodities that did not compete with agriculture in the developed countries. For agriculture and manufactures, developing countries faced severe barriers. Further, most developing countries erected barriers against each other and against developed countries.

The partial reduction in trade barriers was reinforced by continued reductions in transport costs: between 1950 and the late 1970s sea freight charges again fell by a third. Overall, trade doubled relative to world income, approximately recovering the level it had reached during the first wave of globalization. However, the resulting liberalization was very lopsided. For developing countries it restored the North-South pattern of trade—the exchange of manufactures for land-intensive primary commodities—but did not restore the international movements of capital and labor.

By contrast, for rich countries the second wave of globalization was spectacular. The lifting of barriers between them greatly expanded the exchange of manufactures. For the first time international specialization within manufacturing became important, allowing agglomeration and scale economies to be realized. This helped to drive up the incomes of the rich countries relative to the rest.

Economies of agglomeration. The second wave introduced a new type of trade: rich country specialization in manufacturing niches that gained productivity from agglomerated clusters. Most trade between developed countries became determined not by comparative advantage based on differences in factor endowments but by cost savings from agglomeration and scale. Because such cost savings are quite specific to each activity, although each individual industry became more and more concentrated geographically, industry as a whole remained very widely dispersed to avoid costs of congestion.

Firms cluster together, some producing the same thing and others connected by vertical linkages (Fujita, Krugman, and Venables 1999). Japanese auto companies, for example, are well known for wanting certain of their parts suppliers to locate within a short distance of the main assembly plant. As Sutton (2000) describes it: "Two-thirds of manufacturing output consists of intermediate goods, sold by one firm to another. The presence of a rich network of manufacturing firms provides a positive externality to each firm in the system, allowing it to acquire inputs locally, thus reducing the costs of transport, of coordination, of monitoring and of contracting."

Clustering enables greater specialization and thus raises productivity. In turn, it depends upon the ability to trade internationally at low cost. The classic statement of this was indeed Adam Smith's: "The division of labor is limited only by the extent of the market" (*The Wealth of Nations*). Smith argued that a larger market permits a finer division of labor, which in turn facilitates innovation. For example, Sokoloff (1988) shows that as the Erie Canal progressed westward in the first half of the 19th century, patent registrations rose county by county as the canal reached them. This pattern suggests that ideas that were already in people's heads became economically viable through access to a larger market.

However, while agglomeration economies are good news for those in the clusters, they are bad news for those left out. A region may be uncompetitive simply because not enough firms have chosen to locate there. As a result "a 'divided world' may emerge, in which a network of manufacturing firms is clustered in some 'high wage' region, while wages in the remaining regions stay low" (Sutton 2000).

Firms will not shift to a new location until the gap in production costs becomes wide enough to compensate for the loss of agglomeration economies. Yet once firms start to relocate, the movement becomes a cascade: as firms re-base to the new location, it starts to benefit from agglomeration economies.

During the second globalization wave most developing countries did not participate in the growth of global manufacturing and services trade. The combination of persistent trade barriers in developed countries, and poor investment climates and anti-trade policies in developing countries, confined them to dependence on primary commodities. Even by

29

1980 only 25 percent of the merchandise exports of developing countries were manufactured goods.

Cascades of relocation did occur during the second wave, but they were to low-wage areas within developed countries. For example, until 1950 the U.S. textile industry was clustered in the high-wage Northeast. The cost pressure for it to relocate built up gradually as northern wages rose and as institutions and infrastructure improved in southern states. Within a short period in the 1950s the whole industry relocated to the Carolinas.

The effect on inequality and poverty. During globalization's second wave there were effectively two trading systems: the old North-South system, and the new intra-North system.

The intra-North system was quite powerfully equalizing: lower-income industrial countries caught up with higher-income ones. Figure 1.4 shows this pattern of long-term convergence among OECD economies.

Second wave globalization coincided with the growth of policies for redistribution and social protection within developed societies. Not only did inequalities reduce between countries—probably an effect of globalization—but inequality was reduced within countries, probably as a result of these social programs. Figure 1.5 shows the dramatic reduction both in between-country and within-country inequality that occurred in developed countries during the period. The second wave

Figure 1.4   Long-term convergence among OECD countries

Percent annual growth rate 1820–1990

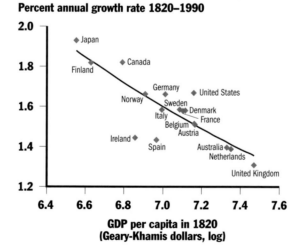

Source: Maddison (1995).

of globalization was thus spectacularly successful in reducing poverty within the OECD countries. Rapid growth coincided with greater equity, both to an extent without precedent. For the industrial world it is often referred to as the "golden age."

Second wave globalization was not golden for developing countries. Although per capita income growth recovered from the inter-war slowdown, it was substantially slower than in the rich economies. The number of poor people continued to rise. Non-income dimensions of poverty improved—notably rising life expectancy and rising school enrollments. In terms of equity, within developing countries in aggregate there was little change either between countries or within them (figure 1.6). As a group, developing countries were being left behind by developed countries.

World inequality was thus the sum of three components: greater equity within developed countries, greater inequality between developed and developing countries, and little net change in developing countries. The net effect of these three very different components was broadly no change. World inequality was about the same in the late 1970s as it had been a quarter of a century earlier (figure 1.7).

The new wave of globalization

THE NEW WAVE OF GLOBALIZATION, WHICH BEGAN ABOUT 1980, is distinctive. First, and most spectacularly, a large group of developing countries broke into global markets. Second, other developing countries became increasingly marginalized in the world economy and suffered declining incomes and rising poverty. Third, international migration and capital movements, which were negligible during second wave globalization, have again become substantial. We take these features of the new global economy in turn.

The changing structure of trade: the rise of the new globalizers

The most encouraging development in third wave globalization is that some developing countries, accounting for about 3 billion people, have succeeded for the first time in harnessing their labor abundance to give them a competitive advantage in labor-intensive manufactures and

Figure 1.5   Household inequality in rich countries, 1960–80

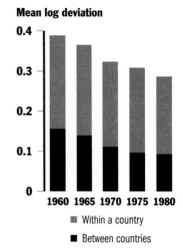

Source: Clark, Dollar, and Kraay (2001).

Figure 1.6   Household inequality in the developing world, 1960–80

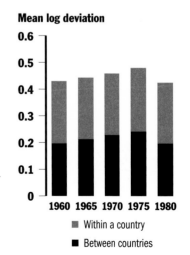

Source: Clark, Dollar, and Kraay (2001).

Figure 1.7 Worldwide household inequality, 1960–79

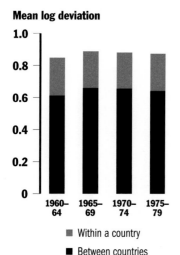

Mean log deviation

■ Within a country
■ Between countries

Source: Clark, Dollar, and Kraay (2001).

services. In 1980 only 25 percent of the exports of developing countries were manufactures; by 1998 this had risen to 80 percent (figure 1.8). Davis and Weinstein (forthcoming) show that developing country exports are indeed now labor-intensive.

This is an astonishing transformation over a very short period. The developing countries that have shifted into manufactures trade are quite diverse. Relatively low-income countries such as China, Bangladesh, and Sri Lanka have manufactures shares in their exports that are above the world average of 81 percent. Others, such as India, Turkey, Morocco, and Indonesia, have shares that are nearly as high as the world average. Another important change in the pattern of developing country exports has been their substantial increase in exports of services. In the early 1980s, commercial services made up 17 percent of the exports of rich countries but only 9 percent of the exports of developing countries. During the third wave of globalization the share of services in rich country exports increased slightly—to 20 percent—but for developing countries the share almost doubled to 17 percent.

What accounted for this shift? Partly it was changing economic policy. Tariffs on manufactured goods in developed countries continued to decline, and many developing countries undertook major trade liberalizations. At the same time many countries liberalized barriers to foreign investment and improved other aspects of their investment climate. Partly it was due to continuing technical progress in transport

Figure 1.8 Shares in merchandise exports in developing country exports

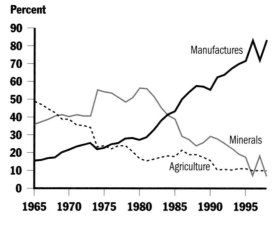

Percent

Source: Martin (2001).

and communications (Venables 2001). Containerization and airfreight brought a considerable speeding up of shipping, allowing countries to participate in international production networks. New information and communications technologies mean it is easier to manage and control geographically dispersed supply chains. And information based activities are "weightless" so their inputs and outputs (digitized information) can be shipped at virtually no cost.

Some analysts have suggested that new technologies lead to the "death of distance" (Cairncross 1997) undermining the advantage of agglomeration. This is likely true in a few activities, while for other activities distance seems to be becoming even more important—for example, the proximity requirements of "just-in time" technologies. The OECD agglomerations continue to have massive cost advantages and technological change may even be increasing these advantages. Even within well-located countries there will be clustering as long as agglomeration economies are important, and hence wage pressure to migrate to towns and cities. For example, within the United States, which has similar institutions across the country, there has been a clear trend for economic activity and labor to migrate away from the center of the country. One hundred years ago the Mississippi River and the Great Lakes provided reasonably good transport links. But recent increases in the scale of ocean-going ships and related declines in ocean shipping rates have increased the competitiveness of U.S. coastal locations compared to the center. It is cheaper to ship iron ore from Australia to Japan than the much shorter distance across the Great Lakes from Minnesota to the steel mills of Illinois and Indiana. For large countries such as China and India we can expect to see more migration toward coastal areas as development proceeds.

By the end of the millennium economic activity was highly concentrated geographically (map 1.1). This reflects differences in policies across countries, natural geographic advantages and disadvantages, and agglomeration and scale economy effects. As the map shows, Africa has a very low output density and this is unlikely to change through a uniform expansion of production in every location. Africa has the potential to develop a number of successful manufacturing/service agglomerations, but if its development is like that of any other large region, there will be several such locations around the continent and a need for labor to migrate to those places. Africa is much less densely populated than Europe, and the importance of migration to create agglomerations is therefore greater.

Map 1.1 GNP density

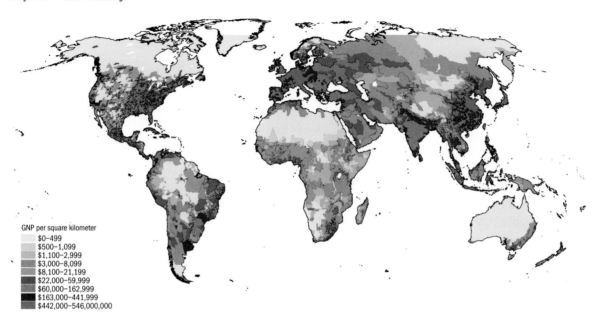

GNP per square kilometer
- $0–499
- $500–1,099
- $1,100–2,999
- $3,000–8,099
- $8,100–21,199
- $22,000–59,999
- $60,000–162,999
- $163,000–441,999
- $442,000–546,000,000

Source: Sachs, Mellinger, and Gallup (2001).

However, most countries are not just victims of their location. The newly globalizing developing countries helped their firms to break into industrial markets by improving the complementary infrastructure, skills and institutions that modern production needs. So, to some extent those developing countries that broke into world markets just happened to be well located, and to some extent they shaped events by their own actions. To get some understanding of this distinction it is useful to look at the characteristics of the post-1980 developing globalizers. We rank developing countries by the extent to which they increased trade relative to income over the period, and compare the top third with the remaining two-thirds. The one-third/two-thirds distinction is of course arbitrary. We label the top third "more globalized" without in any sense implying that they adopted pro-trade policies.[3] The rise in trade may have been due to other policies or even to pure chance. By construction, the "more globalized" had a large increase in trade relative to income: 104 percent, compared to 71 percent for the rich countries. The remaining two-thirds of developing countries have actually had a decline in trade to GDP over this period. The variation in export performance is illustrated in figure 1.9.

The more globalized were not drawn from the higher-income developing countries. Indeed, in 1980 they were poorer as a group.[4] The two groups had very similar educational attainment in 1980 (table 1.1). Since 1980, the more globalized have made very significant gains in basic education: the average years of primary schooling for adults increased from 2.4 years to 3.8 years. The less globalized made less progress and now lag behind in primary attainment. The spread of basic education tends to reduce inequality and raise health standards, as well as being complementary to the process of raising productivity. It can also be seen in table 1.1 that both groups reduced inflation to single digits over the past two decades. Finally, as of 1997 the more globalized fared moderately better on an index of property rights and the rule of law.[5] The same measure is not available for 1980, but clearly countries such as China and Hungary have strengthened property rights as they have reformed.

During third wave globalization, the new globalizers also cut import tariffs significantly, 34 points on average, compared to 11 points for the countries that are less globalized (figure 1.10). However, policy change was not exclusively or even primarily focused on trade. The list of post-1980 globalizers includes such well-known reformers as Argentina,

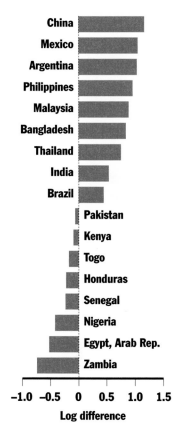

Figure 1.9 Change in trade/GDP for selected countries, 1977–97

Source: World Bank (2001d).

Table 1.1 Characteristics of more globalized and less globalized developing economies
(population-weighted averages)

Socioeconomic characteristics	More globalized (24)	Less globalized (49)
Population, 1997 (billions)	2.9	1.1
Per capita GDP, 1980	$1,488	$1,947
Per capita GDP, 1997	$2,485	$2,133
Inflation, 1980 (percent)	16	17
Inflation, 1997 (percent)	6	9
Rule of law index, 1997 (world average = 0)	−0.04	−0.48
Average years primary schooling, 1980	2.4	2.5
Average years primary schooling, 1997	3.8	3.1
Average years secondary schooling, 1980	0.8	0.7
Average years secondary schooling, 1997	1.3	1.3
Average years tertiary schooling, 1980	0.08	0.09
Average years tertiary schooling, 1997	0.18	0.22

Source: Dollar (2001).

35

Figure 1.10   Decline in average import tariffs, mid-1980s to late-1990s

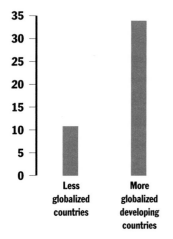

Source: Dollar and Kraay (2001b).

Figure 1.11   Results from a better rule of law

Percentage points of GDP

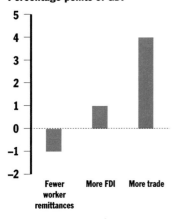

Source: Dollar and Zoido-Lobatón (2001).

China, Hungary, India, Malaysia, Mexico, the Philippines, and Thailand, which undertook reforms involving investment liberalization, stabilization, and property rights. The outcome of increased integration into the world economy need not be due to changes in trade policy. Dollar and Zoido-Lobatón (2001) find that reliable property rights, strong rule of law, and macroeconomic stability are all associated with more trade and FDI. A one standard deviation increase on an index of the rule of law (roughly the difference between Kenya and Uganda) is associated with 4 percentage points of GDP more in trade and 1 percentage point more FDI (figure 1.11). They also find that it is associated with lower emigration.

As they reformed and integrated with the world market, the "more globalized" developing countries started to grow rapidly, accelerating steadily from 2.9 percent in the 1970s to 5 percent through the 1990s (figure 1.12). They found themselves in a virtuous circle of rising growth and rising penetration of world markets. It seems likely that growth and trade reinforced each other, and that the policies of educational expansion, reduced trade barriers, and strategic sectoral reforms reinforced both growth and trade.

Whether there is a causal connection from opening up trade to faster growth is not the issue. In those low-income countries that have broken into global markets, more restricted access to those markets would be damaging to growth, regardless of whether industrialization was triggered by opening up. However, opening up integrates an economy into a larger market, and from Adam Smith on economists have suggested that the size of the market matters for growth. A larger market gives access to more ideas, allows for investment in large fixed-cost investments and enables a finer division of labor. A larger market also widens choice. Wider choice for high-income consumers is irrelevant for poverty reduction, but wider choice may have mattered more for firms than for consumers. For example, as India liberalized trade, companies were able to purchase better-quality machine tools. Similar effects have been found for the Chinese import liberalization. Finally, a larger market intensifies competition and this can spur innovation. There is some evidence that integration with the world economy is more important for small and poor economies than it is for large economies like India and China (Sachs and Warner 1995; Collier and Gunning 1999).

There is also a large amount of cross-country regression evidence on openness and growth (see box 1.1). This should be treated with caution but not dismissed altogether. Lindert and Williamson (2001a) summarize it:

The doubts that one can retain about each individual study threaten to block our view of the overall forest of evidence. Even though no one study can establish that openness to trade has unambiguously helped the representative Third World economy, the preponderance of evidence supports this conclusion. One way to see the whole forest more clearly is to consider two sets, one almost empty and one completely empty. The almost-empty set consists of all statistical studies showing that protection has helped Third World economic growth, and liberalization has harmed it. The second, and this time empty, set contains those countries that chose to be less open to trade and factor flows in the 1990s than in the 1960s and rose in the global living-standard ranks at the same time. As far as we can tell, there are no anti-global victories to report for the postwar Third World. We infer that this is because freer trade stimulates growth in Third World economies today, regardless of its effects before 1940. (pp. 29–30)

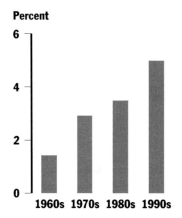

Figure 1.12 Per capita GDP growth rates: more globalized developing countries

Source: Dollar and Kraay (2001b).

Box 1.1 Openness and growth: Regression evidence

IT IS DIFFICULT TO ESTABLISH A LINK BETWEEN openness and growth in a rigorous manner. The specific trade liberalization actions that are important often include non-tariff measures such as eliminating licensing schemes or allowing access to foreign exchange for current account transactions, and it is difficult to quantify these policies. Further, countries tend to pursue a broad package of reforms at the same time so that identifying the separate effect of one reform may not be possible. Recognizing these limitations, what does the cross-country literature find? Sachs and Warner (1995) claim that liberal trade policies cause growth. They develop a measure of openness based on tariff rates for capital equipment, the extent of non-tariff barriers, and the degree of distortion in the foreign exchange market (proxied by the parallel market premium). Dollar (1992) creates

an index of the price level adjusted for factor endowments, arguing that high prices for tradable goods reflect high levels of import protection, and finds a significant effect on growth. Both measures have been criticized (by Rodriguez and Rodrik 1999, among others) on the grounds that they are more a measure of good institutions and policies in general than of trade policy narrowly defined. This points up an important identification problem: the countries with more open trade and investment policies tend to be ones with more reliable property rights and better economic institutions more generally. Frankel and Romer (1999) find that openness as measured by the share of trade in income is robustly related to long-term growth. They are able to rule out the possibility of reverse causation from growth to trade by "instrumenting" for trade with geography variables.

(box countinues on following page)

37

Box 1.1 continued

While this is supportive of models in which access to markets accelerates growth, there is no easy way to rule out the possibility that geography matters for growth through other channels. A different approach to measuring openness is taken by Ades and Glaeser (1999) in their study of 19th century America. They focus on openness in the sense of access to seaports and rail services, and find that backward, open regions tend to grow fast and converge on more advanced regions. Specifically, they interact their openness measure with the initial level of development and find that the combination of openness and backwardness is associated with especially rapid development. Finally, there are some recent studies that focus on changes in growth rates and changes in trade and FDI. This approach has the advantage that all of the variables that do not change over time drop out of the analysis (geography, ethnolinguistic fractionalization, institutional measures that show no time variation), reducing the multicollinearity problems. Dollar and Kraay (2001b) show that both increased trade and increased FDI are related to accelerated growth. They control for changes in other policies and address reverse causation with internal instruments.

To conclude, since 1980 the global integration of markets in merchandise has enabled those developing countries with reasonable locations, policies, institutions, and infrastructure to harness their abundant labor to give themselves a competitive advantage in some manufactures and services. The initial advantage provided by cheap labor has sometimes triggered a virtuous circle of other benefits from trade. For example, when Bangalore initially broke into the world software market, it did so by harnessing its comparative advantage in cheap, educated labor. As more firms gravitated to the city it began to reap economies of agglomeration. The increased export earnings financed more imports, thereby both intensifying competition and widening choice. There is some evidence that between them these four effects of trade raise not only the level of real income, but also its rate of growth. However, the growth process is complex. Trade is certainly not sufficient for growth.

Marginalization: Why has the experience of many poor countries been the opposite of the globalizers?

Countries with total populations of around 2 billion people have not integrated strongly into the global industrial economy. They include most of Africa and many of the economies of the FSU. These countries often suffered deteriorating and volatile terms of trade in the markets for their primary commodity exports. In aggregate their per capita income actually declined during the third wave. Why did these countries diverge so drastically from the globalizers? Can they belatedly emulate the globalizers in harnessing their comparative advantage in abundant labor, thereby diversifying their exports toward services and manufactures? There are three views:

The "Join the Club" view. This view argues that weak globalizers have failed to harness their comparative advantage in abundant labor because of poor economic policies. If, for example, infrastructure is poor, education is inadequate, corruption is rampant, and trade barriers are high, then the cost advantage from abundant labor might be more than offset by these disadvantages. According to this view, as and when policies, institutions, and infrastructure are improved, then countries will integrate into world markets for manufactures and services.

The "Geographic Disadvantage" view. This view argues that many of the countries that have failed to enter global manufacturing markets suffer from fundamental disadvantages of location. Even with good policies, institutions, and infrastructure, a landlocked, malaria-infested country simply will not be competitive in manufacturing or in services such as tourism. It is sometimes argued that it is precisely because the benefits of good policies, institutions, and infrastructure in such environments are so modest that they are not reformed.

For many developing countries, transport costs to OECD markets are higher than the tariffs on their goods, so that transport costs are even more of a barrier to integration than the trade policies of rich countries. Sometimes the explanation for high transport costs is indeed adverse geography. But transport costs are also heavily influenced by the quality of infrastructure as implied by the "Join the Club" view. Limão and Venables (2000) find that "African economies tend to trade less with the rest of the world and with themselves than would be predicted by a simple gravity model, and the reason for that is their poor infrastructure" (p. 25). That includes inefficient seaports, but even more importantly the internal infrastructure of roads, rail, and telecommunications. Collier and Gunning (1999, pp. 71–72) document these infrastructure deficiencies in Africa:

> There is less infrastructure than elsewhere. For example, the density of the rural road network is only 55 kilometers per thousand

square kilometers, compared to over 800 in India, and there are only one-tenth the telephones per capita of Asia. The quality of infrastructure is also lower. The telephone system has triple the level of faults to Asia's and the proportion of diesel trains in use is 40 percent lower. Prices of infrastructure use are much higher. Freight rates by rail are on average around double those in Asia. Port charges are higher (for example, a container costs $200 in Abidjan as opposed to $120 in Antwerp). Air transportation is four times more costly than in East Asia. Much of international transport is cartelized, reflecting the regulations of African governments intended to promote national shipping companies and airlines. As a result of these high costs, by 1991 freight and insurance payments on trade amounted to 15 percent of export earnings, whereas the average for developing countries is only 6 percent. Further, the trend has been rising for Africa whereas it has been falling elsewhere: the comparable figures for 1970 were 11 percent and 8 percent.

Thus, many of the weak globalizers have high transport costs to world markets partly due to intrinsically poor location and partly due to bad infrastructure. As a result they will have low wages, and even when trade is free of barriers it will not bring those wages into line with wages in more favored locations.

The "Missed the Boat" view. This view accepts the argument of the "Join the Club" view that, if any of these countries had had good policies it would have broken into world manufacturing and services, but it further argues that most of them have now missed the boat. World demand for manufactures is limited by world income, and because of agglomeration economies firms will locate in clusters. Although there is room for many clusters, firms already have satisfactory locations in labor-abundant countries and so the latecomers have nothing to offer.

Who's right?

Most plausibly, each view is right to some extent. It seems highly likely that there will be room for some new entrants to the market for global manufactures and services, and some well-located cities in countries that reform their policies, institutions, and infrastructure will surely develop successful clusters. Equally, it seems plausible that if all countries reformed, there would be more well-located sites than new clusters, so some would indeed have missed the boat. Finally, some countries are indeed badly located and will simply not industrialize. Such countries might become competitive in international services, but at present markets in services are far less integrated than markets in merchandise. This is partly because until very recently trade negotiations have focused on reducing barriers to merchandise trade.

Regardless of whether the disadvantages faced by the weak globalizers were intrinsic or could have been altered by better policy, their growth rates were even lower during third wave globalization than during the second wave. One reason is that many countries dependent on primary commodities suffered declining prices for their exports. This was probably related to the slowdown in growth in developed countries. Could globalization itself have contributed to the economic marginalization of some countries? One way it might have adversely affected the weak globalizers is through the growth of international capital markets. Most marginalized countries integrated into world capital markets not through attracting capital inflows but through capital flight. By 1990 Africa, the region where capital is most scarce, had about 40 percent of its private wealth held outside the continent, a higher proportion than any other region. This integration was not a policy choice: most African governments erected capital controls, but they were ineffective. The main drivers of capital flight have been exchange rate misalignment, poor risk-ratings, and high indebtedness (Collier, Hoeffler, and Patillo 2001). However, capital flight was probably eased by the growth of international banking, some of it offshore, with poor practices of disclosure. A second way that globalization may have affected the weak globalizers adversely is through a rising risk of civil war. The incidence of civil war has declined sharply in the globalizing developing regions, but has risen sharply in Africa. Dependence on primary commodity exports is a powerful risk factor in civil conflict, probably because it provides easy sources of finance for rebel groups. Whereas most regions have diversified their exports, Africa has remained heavily dependent on primary commodities. Furthermore, conflicts tend to last longer: the chances of reaching peace are much lower during third wave globalization than during the second wave.

The re-emergence of international capital flows

Controls on capital outflows from high-income countries were gradually lifted: for example, the United Kingdom removed capital controls in 1979. Governments in developing countries have also gradually adopted less hostile policies toward investors. Partly as a result of these policy changes and partly due to the oil shock of the 1970s, significant amounts of private capital again began to flow to developing countries.

Total capital flows to developing countries went from less than $28 billion in the 1970s to about $306 billion in 1997, in real terms (figure 1.13), when they peaked. In the process, their composition changed significantly. The importance of official flows of aid more than halved, while private capital flows became the major source of capital for a number of emerging economies. The composition of private capital flows also changed markedly. FDI grew continuously throughout the 1990s. Mergers and acquisitions were the most important source of this increase, especially those resulting from the privatization of public companies. Net portfolio flows grew from $0.01 billion in 1970 to $103 billion in 1996, in real terms. New international mutual funds and pension funds helped to channel the equity flows to developing countries. The importance of syndicated bank loans and other private flows decreased steadily in relative terms throughout this period, especially after the debt crises of the 1980s.

Even though net private capital flows to developing countries increased during the third wave of globalization, by one measure they remained

Figure 1.13   Net capital flows to developing countries by type of flow, 1970–98

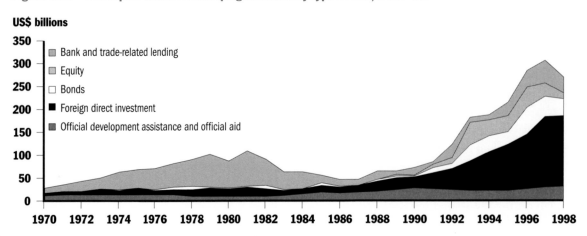

US$ billions

Legend:
- Bank and trade-related lending
- Equity
- Bonds
- Foreign direct investment
- Official development assistance and official aid

Source: Schmukler and Zoido-Lobatón (2001).

more modest than during the first wave. By 1998 the foreign capital stock was 22 percent of developing country GDP, roughly double what it had been in the mid-1970s but still well below the 32 percent reached in 1914 (Maddison 2001). Some countries receive large inflows, while other countries receive little. The top 12 emerging markets are receiving the overwhelming majority of the net inflows—countries such as Argentina, Brazil, China, India, Malaysia, Mexico, and Thailand. Much the most successful developing countries in attracting FDI were Malaysia and Chile, both with stocks of FDI of about $2,000 per capita.

FDI brings not just capital, but also advanced technology and access to international markets. It is critical for participating in international production networks. Dollar and Kraay (2001b) find that FDI has a powerful growth effect, whereas the overall level of investment by itself does not have a significant effect on growth—other factors are more important.

Capital flows to developing countries are just a tiny proportion of the global capital market. Because capital owners are concerned about risk, most global capital flows are between developed countries rather than from developed to developing countries. Even Malaysia and Chile have less FDI per capita than any of the major developed economies. FDI per capita in the United States is more than $3,200 per capita, while in Africa it is only $124 (Maddison 2001). This is despite the fact that differences in capital per member of the labor force between developed and developing countries are now far larger than they were during the first wave of globalization. World capital markets could clearly do more to raise growth in low-income countries. As we discuss in Chapter 3, there is evidence of systematic bias against Africa.

Migration pressures are building

The massive gaps in income that had built up by the end of globalization's second wave created intense economic pressures for people to migrate out of poor areas—both rural-urban migration within countries and international migration. These pressures were largely frustrated by immigration controls, but in some rich countries controls were somewhat relaxed during the third wave, with powerful effects on wages in poor countries.

Recall that in the first great wave of modern globalization, from 1870 to 1910, about 10 percent of the world's population relocated permanently. Much of this flow was driven by economic considerations, the desire to find a better life in a more favorable location. The same forces operate today, though policies toward international migration are much more restrictive than in the past. About 120 million people (2 percent of the world's population) live in foreign countries (that is, not in the country of their citizenship). Roughly half of this stock of migrants is in the industrial countries and half in the developing world. However, because the population of developing countries is about five times greater than the population of the developed countries, migrants comprise a larger share of the population in rich countries (about 6 percent) than in poor countries (about 1 percent).

The main economic rationale for migration is that wages for the same skills differ vastly in different locations, especially between developing countries and rich ones. The average hourly labor compensation in manufacturing is about $30 per hour in Germany, and one one-hundredth of that level (30 cents) in China and India (figure 1.14). That gap is particularly extreme, but even between the United States and newly industrialized countries such as Thailand or Malaysia the compensation gap is ten-fold. Now, some of that difference results from the fact that the typical German worker has quite a bit more education and training than the typical Chinese or Indian. However, skill differences can only explain a small amount of the wage differential. A study following individual, legal immigrants found that on average they left jobs in Mexico paying $31 per week and on arrival in the United States could immediately earn $278 per week (a nine-fold increase). Similarly, Indonesian workers in Indonesia earn 28 cents per day, compared to $2 per day or more in next-door Malaysia. Clearly there are huge real gains to individual workers who migrate to more developed economies.

These large wage differentials across countries lead to mounting migration pressures, although the actual scale of migration depends upon the entry restrictions that migrants face. Hatton and Williamson (2001) study emigration from Africa. They find that both widening wage differentials and a demographic bulge of 15–29-year-olds are producing large and growing economic pressure for migration, although so far much of this has been bottled up by entry restrictions. Emigration from Mexico has been less restricted. There are about 7 million legal Mexican migrants living in the United States, and an additional estimated 3 million undocumented workers. This means that about 10

Figure 1.14   Hourly labor costs in manufacturing

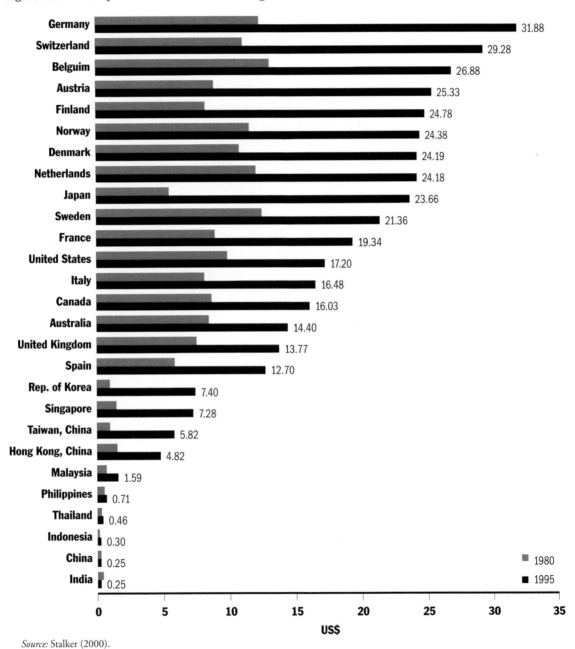

Source: Stalker (2000).

percent of Mexico's population is living and working in the United States. Emigration on this scale has a significant effect on developing country labor markets. Hatton and Williamson estimate the effect of out-migration from Africa on the wages of those who remain behind. They find that emigration powerfully raises the wages of remaining unskilled workers. It is likely that emigration from Mexico has substantially raised Mexican wages.

The benefits of migration to the sending region go beyond the higher wages for those who remain behind. Migrants send a large volume of remittances back to relatives and this is an important source of capital inflows (figure 1.15). India receives six times as much in remittances from its workers overseas every year as it gets in foreign aid.

Further, much trade and investment depends on personal and family networks. To take a significant historical example, a large number of Chinese have emigrated from China to other Asian countries (especially Thailand, Malaysia, Indonesia, and Singapore). The Chinese family networks play a significant role in trade and investment between these countries and China. It is inherently difficult to study and quantify this phenomenon, but there is more general evidence that language plays a large role in explaining trade and investment flows, and it makes sense that the stronger tie of family and kinship would have an even greater effect. The point here is that migration can facilitate the other flows of globalization—trade, capital, and ideas. Take, for example, the recent surge in Indian immigration to the United States. It happens that this immigration is particularly related to the high-tech sectors. It will support greater flows of technology and information between the United States and India, and also encourage more U.S. investment in India. Some successful Indian entrepreneurs in the United States may themselves open plants back in their home country, or U.S. companies may hire Indian engineers to work in India. And because much of manufacturing and services trade is associated with these kinds of networks, trade between the two countries is likely to increase.

What have been the effects of third wave globalization on income distribution and poverty?

The breakthrough of developing countries into global markets for manufactures and services, and the re-emergence of migration and capital flows,

Figure 1.15   Workers' remittances, 1999

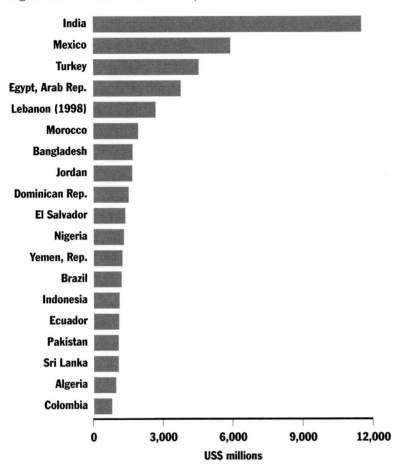

Source: World Bank (2001d).

have affected poverty and the distribution of income between and within countries. Domestic policy choices unrelated to globalization also affect income distribution.

Among developed countries globalization has continued to generate the convergence of the first and second waves. By 1995 inequality between countries was less than half what it had been in 1960 and substantially less than it had been in 1980. However, as figure 1.16 shows, there was a serious offsetting increase in inequality within individual countries, reversing the trend seen during the second wave. A part of this may have been due to immigration. However, it may also have been

Figure 1.16   Household inequality in rich countries, 1980–95

Mean log deviation

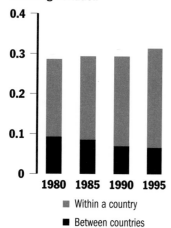

Source: Clark, Dollar, and Kraay (2001).

Figure 1.17   Household inequality in the globalizing world, 1975–95

Mean log deviation

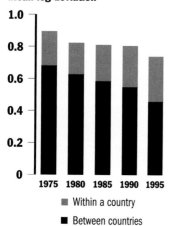

Source: Clark, Dollar, and Kraay (2001).

due to policy changes on taxation and social spending unconnected to globalization. Global economic integration is consistent with wide differences in domestic distributional policies: inequality differs massively between equally globalized economies. For the OECD economies taken as a whole, globalization has probably been equalizing as inequality between countries has radically decreased.

Among the new globalizers the same pattern of convergence has been evident as has occurred among the OECD economies over a longer period. Sachs and Warner (1995) find that this is indeed a general phenomenon among open economies. Treating the OECD and the new globalizers as a common group of integrated economies, overall inequality has declined (figure 1.17).

As in the OECD countries, within-country inequality has increased in the new globalizers. However, this is entirely due to the rise in inequality in China, which alone accounts for one-third of the population of the new globalizers. China started its modernization with an extremely equal distribution of income and extremely high poverty. Intra-rural inequality in China has actually decreased. The big growth in inequality has been between the rural areas and the rising urban agglomerations (figure 1.18), and between those provinces with agglomerations and those without them.

A closer investigation of the changes in inequality within countries is provided in Dollar and Kraay (2001a) and Ravallion (forthcoming). There are substantial difficulties in comparing income distribution data across countries. Countries differ in the concept measured (income versus consumption), the measure of income (gross versus net), the unit of observation (individuals versus households), and the coverage of the survey (national versus subnational). Dollar and Kraay restrict attention to distribution data based on nationally representative sources identified as high-quality by Deininger and Squire (1996), and perform some simple adjustments to control for differences in the types of surveys. These data cover a total of 137 countries. They focus on what has happened to the income of the poorest 20 percent of the population. They find that on average there is a one-to-one relationship between the growth rate of income of the poor and the growth rate of average income in society. However, there is much variation around that average relationship. They then investigate whether changes in trade account for any of this variation. They find no relationship between changes in openness and changes in

Figure 1.18 Increased inequality in China reflecting growing inequality among locations

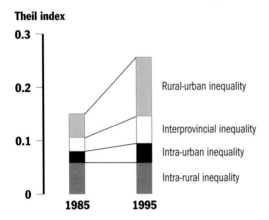

Theil index

Rural-urban inequality

Interprovincial inequality

Intra-urban inequality

Intra-rural inequality

1985   1995

Source: Nehru (1997).

inequality, whether openness is measured by the share of trade in income, the Sachs-Warner measure of openness, average tariff rates, or capital controls. Ravallion qualifies this result. He finds that although *on average* openness does not affect inequality, in low-income countries it is associated with greater inequality. Regardless of its net effect, there are winners and losers from trade policies.

The combination of rapid growth with no systematic change in inequality has dramatically reduced absolute poverty in the new globalizing countries. Between 1993 and 1998 (the most recent period for which we have data) the number of people in absolute poverty declined by 14 percent to 762 million. For them, the third wave of globalization is indeed the golden age. Poverty is predominantly rural. As the new globalizers have broken into world markets their pace of industrialization and urbanization has increased. People have taken the opportunity to migrate from risky and impoverished rural livelihoods to less vulnerable and better paid jobs in towns and cities. Not only has poverty declined viewed in terms of income, but other dimensions of poverty have rapidly improved. Both average years of schooling and life expectancy have improved to levels close or equal to levels reached by the rich countries in 1960. Vietnam illustrates this experience. As it has integrated into the world economy, it has had a large increase in per capita income and no significant change in inequality. The income of the poor has risen dramatically, and the level of absolute poverty has dropped sharply, from 75 percent of the population in 1988 to 37 percent in 1998. Poverty was cut in half in only 10 years. We can be unusually confident of this information because a representative household survey was conducted early in the reform process (1992–93), and the same 5,000 households were visited again six years later. Of the poorest 5 percent of households in 1992, 98 percent had higher incomes six years later. Vietnam was unusually successful in entering global markets for labor-intensive products such as footwear, and the increased employment might be expected to benefit poor households. Uganda had a similar experience: dramatic poverty reduction and no increase in inequality.

While the more globalized economies grew and converged, the less globalized developing economies declined and diverged. Their growth experience was worse than during the second wave, but their divergence has been longstanding. Ades and Glaeser (1999) find that at least since 1960, less globalized developing countries, defined by the share of trade in income, have tended to diverge. Decline and divergence had severe consequences for poverty in its various dimensions. Between 1993 and 1998 the number of people in absolute poverty in the less globalized developing countries rose by 4 percent to 437 million. Not only were per capita incomes falling, but in many countries life expectancy and school enrollments declined.

During the second wave of globalization the rich countries diverged from the poor countries, a trend that had persisted for a century. During the third wave the new globalizers have started to catch up with the rich countries, while the weak globalizers are falling further behind.

The change in the overall distribution of world income and the number of poor people are thus the net outcomes of offsetting effects. Among rich countries there has been convergence: the less rich countries have caught up with the richest, while within some rich countries there has been rising inequality. Among the new globalizers there has also been convergence and falling poverty. Within China there has also been rising inequality, but not on average elsewhere. Between the rich countries and the new globalizers there has been convergence. Between all these groups and the weak globalizers there has been divergence. The net effect is that the long trend of rising global inequality and rising numbers of people in absolute poverty has been halted and even reversed (figure 1.19). Bourguignon and Morrisson (2001) estimate that the number of people in absolute poverty fell by about 100 million between 1980 and 1992 (the endpoint of their analysis). Chen and Ravallion (2001) estimate that there was a further fall of about 100 million between 1993 (the closest date for comparison) and 1998.

Thus, globalization clearly can be a force for poverty reduction. In subsequent chapters we look at important factors at the global and local level that will determine whether it continues to be so. The next chapter takes up the global architecture for flows of goods, capital, and people, focusing on measures to strengthen integration and to enable locations currently left out of globalization to participate and benefit. Chapter 3 then turns to the national and local agenda in developing countries. Chapter 4 takes up issues of power, culture, and the environment. Chapter 5 brings together and summarizes the agenda for action to make globalization work better for poor countries and poor people.

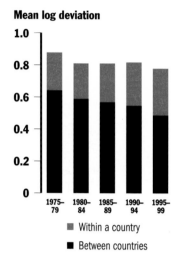

Figure 1.19 Worldwide household inequality, 1975–99

Mean log deviation

- Within a country
- Between countries

Source: Clark, Dollar, and Kraay (2001).

Notes

1.   Much of the emigration from India was forced, rather than voluntary.

2.   The mean log deviation has the advantage that it can be decomposed into inequality between locations and inequality within locations. It also has an intuitive interpretation. Income distributions everywhere are skewed in favor of the rich, so that the "typical" person (one chosen randomly from the population) has less income than the average for the whole group. Roughly speaking, the mean log deviation (times 100) is the percent gap between the typical person and the average income. The more skewed the distribution in favor of the rich, the larger is this gap. So, for example, if per capita income in the world is around $5,000 and the median person is living on $1,000 (80 percent less), the mean log deviation will be around 0.8.

3.   For this calculation we separated out rich economies (the original members of the OECD plus Chile; Korea; Singapore; Taiwan,China; and Hong Kong, China). The "more globalized"—the top third of developing countries in terms of increased trade to GDP between the 1970s and the 1990s—are Argentina, Bangladesh, Brazil, China,

Colombia, Costa Rica, Côte d'Ivoire, the Dominican Republic, Haiti, Hungary, India, Jamaica, Jordan, Malaysia, Mali, Mexico, Nepal, Nicaragua, Paraguay, the Philippines, Rwanda, Thailand, Uruguay, and Zimbabwe. The "less globalized" are all other developing countries for which we have data. The less globalized group is a very diverse set of countries. It includes failed states whose economic performance has been extremely poor. It also includes some countries of the former Soviet Union that went through a difficult transition in the 1990s. Some of the less globalized countries have had stable but not increasing trade, and positive but slow growth.

4.   The more globalized had per capita GDP, at purchasing power parity, of $1,488 in 1980, compared to $1,947 for other developing countries (table 1.1). These are population-weighted averages so that relatively poor China and India have a large weight. However, even a simple average of GDP per capita was significantly lower for the globalizers in 1980.

5.   The rule of law index has a standard deviation of 1.0. The 0.44 advantage of the globalizers is roughly the same as Uganda's advantage over Zambia on this measure.

CHAPTER TWO

Improving the International Architecture for Integration

O NE OF THE DISTINCTIVE FEATURES OF THE current wave of globalization is that many developing countries are participating actively— more than they did in the past. This greater participation comes partly from unilateral moves toward more open trade and investment policies. But developing countries are also playing a more active role in the multilateral institutions that govern international trade and investment. This chapter focuses on the prospects for growing trade, investment, and labor integration between rich and poor countries, and how the international architecture can be improved to support that integration.

The first section focuses on trade policies. The Uruguay Round was quite different from earlier multilateral negotiations in the number of agreements that required developing countries to develop or upgrade their trade-related institutions. Developing countries made a "grand bargain," in which they further lowered tariffs on manufactured products and adopted standards for Intellectual Property Rights (IPRs) in exchange for the abolition of rich country quotas on textiles and clothing, the introduction of more effective disciplines on agriculture, and abolition of Voluntary Export Restraints (VERs). Developing countries have been disappointed that the rich countries have been slow to follow through on their commitments to dismantle textile quotas and to reduce agricultural protection. A conservative estimate of the cost to poor countries of rich country protection is $100 billion per year, about twice the total volume of foreign aid they receive. Developing countries also maintain significant trade barriers—70 percent of the tariff barriers that developing countries face are in other developing countries. There would be large gains from a round of trade negotiations focused on market access in goods and services.

Experiences with international capital flows are taken up in the following section. Hand-in-hand with trade liberalization, developing countries have reduced restrictions on foreign investment. Private capital flows to developing countries—especially FDI—have soared. FDI both increases the supply of capital and provides access to technology. While private flows have risen dramatically, official development assistance from industrial countries to developing ones has declined. For poor areas that do not now benefit much from globalization, there is a need for more aid, better managed. There has also been a more erratic increase in private financial flows—bank lending, bonds, and equity. These flows bring risks. We consider how the international community can better manage them. The process of opening up increases risks and has all too frequently been accompanied by devastating financial and exchange rate crises, although if countries can get through this stage their risk falls back to what it was before opening. Countries that are not yet fully open—such as China and India—should approach financial opening with caution. Good macro fundamentals and micro fundamentals (supervision and regulation of the financial system) are prerequisites to successful financial opening. Foreign investment in financial and accounting services can help with the needed strengthening. Even with the best of institutions and policies, countries can be buffeted by international financial crises because these markets are subject to irrational boom and bust cycles. Better international coordination is needed on accounting standards and transparency and on the management of incipient financial crises. This should be done in such a way that adequate liquidity is ensured for countries with sound policies, while at the same time private investors are discouraged from and penalized for risky lending practices.

The final section focuses on migration from developing to industrial countries, and among the developing countries themselves. While migration could make a large contribution to poverty reduction, OECD immigration policies are highly restrictive and often encourage "brain drain" migration of highly skilled workers from the South, while shutting off legal flows of unskilled workers. It is understandable that migration is the most controversial of the flows arising from globalization. There is evidence that migration reduces the relative wages of unskilled workers in industrial countries, and also has effects on society and culture that some people value and others find threatening. Nevertheless, demographics will lead to growing pressure for migration of unskilled workers. Most of the increase in the labor force in the next 15 years will occur in the regions where poverty is now concentrated: South Asia and Sub-Saharan Africa. In Europe and Japan, the labor force will shrink without greater migration, and the ratio of workers to retirees will rise sharply, putting extreme pressure on social security systems. There would be large mutual benefits from more migration of unskilled workers from locations with an oversupply of labor to those with an undersupply.

Trade policy

AVERAGE TARIFF RATES IN DEVELOPING COUNTRIES HAVE BEEN cut in half, from around 30 percent in the early 1980s to about 15 percent in the late 1990s (figure 2.1). The absolute reductions in tariff rates in developing countries have been much higher than in industrial countries and decreases from a higher level are likely to have a much greater welfare benefit than corresponding decreases from a lower base (Martin 1997). In addition, the dispersion of tariff rates, which typically increases the welfare cost of any given average tariff rate, was substantially reduced. Reductions have been particularly large in South Asia, Latin America, and East Asia. Trade liberalization has been more limited in Sub-Saharan Africa and in the Middle East and North Africa.

Figure 2.1 Average unweighted tariff rates by region

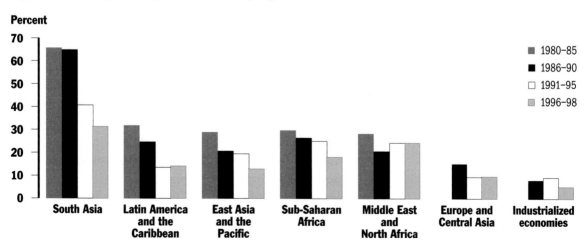

Source: World Bank (2001d).

Along with these reductions in tariffs, the coverage of quotas fell sharply and foreign exchange restrictions were reduced, so that trade liberalization took place across a wide front.

The result of this trade liberalization in the developing world has been a large increase in both imports and exports. Developing countries in this more open environment are increasingly exporting labor-intensive manufactures. As recently as 1980 manufactured goods made up only a quarter of exports from developing countries. That share has increased steadily during the third wave of globalization, reaching more than 80 percent in 1998. Along with the changes in the commodity composition of exports have come substantial changes in the direction of exports. During the second wave less than 20 percent of developing country exports were destined for other developing countries. By 1995, this had increased to more than 40 percent. This increase in the importance of developing countries as markets for each others' goods results from a number of factors, including growth in the share of developing countries in the world economy and the liberalization of developing country trade. With 40 percent of their exports going to other developing countries, the barriers that these countries face from each other are clearly more important than they once were. More than 70 percent of the tariff burden faced by manufactured goods from developing countries is now imposed by other developing countries (Hertel and Martin 2001).

The dramatic increase in exports of manufactures from developing countries has contributed to protectionist concerns in both industrial and developing countries, and to the emergence of new concerns about such issues as labor standards. With so many developing nations emerging as important trading countries, reaching further agreements on multilateral trade liberalization has become more complicated.

The Uruguay Round ushered in a new era of multilateral trade negotiations (Martin and Winters 1996). For the first time, developing countries engaged comprehensively in the core business of the WTO, the exchange of market access concessions. Developing countries were willing to "bind" their tariffs on 100 percent of their agricultural imports and on more than 60 percent of their imports of industrial products (Abreu 1996).[1] Developing countries played a pivotal role in ensuring that agriculture was returned to GATT disciplines, that VERs were abolished, and that the highly protectionist quota regime for textiles and clothing would be phased out. To do this, they agreed to a "grand bargain," in which intellectual property protection of primary interest to the rich countries was introduced. The coverage of trade agreements was also extended to services, and many disciplines that had previously applied only to members of plurilateral agreements were brought within the "single undertaking" of the Uruguay Round. The WTO was established and given a much stronger system for dispute resolution.

For developing countries, an important development that was perhaps not sufficiently noted at the time was the increase in requirements for deeper integration—that is, rules that require the strengthening of institutions to bring them into effect. This was most noticeable in the case of trade-related intellectual property (TRIPs), but also in areas such as the agreement on customs valuation. As Finger and Schuler (2001) have pointed out, the costs of implementing these agreements can be substantial.

Despite the dramatic increases in the size of the membership, and in the coverage of the multilateral system with formation of the WTO, relatively few changes were made in the operation of the trading system. The consensus principle is still used for major decisions, and all members are represented equally on the executive governing body, the general council, as well as at ministerial meetings. While this gives smaller developing countries much more representation than they would have with a smaller executive body, they have much less influence than the equality of representation would imply. Logistical difficulties mean that many developing countries are inadequately represented in Geneva, and hence unable to participate fully in the wide range of WTO activities (Blackhurst, Lyakurwa, and Oyejide 2001). Further, size matters in many cases, particularly in areas such as dispute settlement, where only larger countries can effectively threaten to retaliate against illegal measures. The power imbalance would be even worse if there was no WTO, because then small countries like Bangladesh would have to negotiate one-on-one with the United States without a multilateral set of rules. Still, it is important to keep in mind that developing countries have difficulty defending their legitimate interests in the WTO, and this difficulty is one reason why they generally oppose expanding the organization's mandate to take up non-trade issues such as labor and environmental standards.

Improved market access

The WTO has the potential to launch a "development round" of trade negotiations at its Doha ministerial meeting (see Hoekman and Martin 2001 and www.worldbank.org/trade for suggestions on what this might include). A central objective of such a round should be improved market access for developing countries. There would be large mutual gains to improved access. We use a model to estimate these gains that is part of the Global Trade Analysis Project (GTAP). It provides a lower-bound estimate of the gains because its assumptions are deliberately conservative. First, it assumes that the developed countries have already fully honored their commitments under the Uruguay Round—notably the abolition of textile quotas. Second, it ignores benefits due to scale effects and dynamics. Third, it ignores benefits from the abolition of anti-dumping duties, "safeguards," excessive standards barriers, and similar trade restrictions. Fourth, it ignores benefits from liberalization of trade in services. It is difficult to quantify the extent to which the model underestimates the likely benefits, but what has been left out may in fact yield even larger potential gains than what has been captured. With these limitations, the results provide some guidance as to what types of trade liberalization offer the largest gains to developing countries.

Developing countries need better access to rich-country markets for manufactured goods. Despite the substantial liberalization of developed country markets for manufactures, developing countries have most to gain from further liberalization of these markets. The model estimates presented in table 2.1 report an annual gain to developing countries from unrestricted access to the developed country markets in textiles and clothing of $9 billion. Recall that this already assumes that the textile quota restrictions have been completely lifted. The gain from unrestricted access to the developed country markets for other manufactures would be

Table 2.1   Potential annual gains from improving market access in a new Development Round, 1995
(US$ billions)

Benefiting region	Liberalizing region	Textiles and clothing	Other manufactures	Agriculture and food	Other primary markets	Total
Developing countries	Rich	9.0	22.3	11.6	0.1	43.0
	Developing	3.6	27.6	31.4	2.5	65.1
	Total	12.6	49.9	43.0	2.6	108.1
Rich countries	Rich	−5.7	−8.1	110.5	0.0	96.7
	Developing	10.5	27.7	11.2	0.2	49.6
	Total	4.8	19.6	121.7	0.2	146.3
All countries	Rich	3.3	14.2	122.1	0.1	139.7
	Developing	14.1	55.3	42.6	2.7	114.7
	Total	17.4	69.5	164.7	2.8	254.4

Source: Anderson and others (2000).

$22.3 billion. Thus, the rise of manufactured exports from developing countries has made this a priority issue for developing countries. It was not part of the built-in agenda from the Uruguay Round, and hence preparations for negotiations on manufactures have not yet commenced, but the issues involved in manufactures trade are, in many respects, much simpler than those involved in either agriculture or services.

Developing countries need better access to rich-country markets for agricultural products. The model estimates that the gains to developing countries from unrestricted access to the agricultural markets of developed countries and abolition of rich-country export subsidies would be $11.6 billion per year. While the potential benefits are substantial, there are major controversies. The countries with high agricultural protection, mostly industrial countries in Europe and East Asia, find themselves aligned against a North-South coalition of agricultural exporting countries. There are major controversies about whether the goal is complete liberalization, including elimination of agricultural subsidies. Another major source of discord is whether non-trade concerns, frequently labeled *multifunctionality* by the protecting countries, should be allowed to affect protection levels. In addition, there are new agriculture-related controversies about biotechnology and whether imports could be restricted under the so-called precautionary principle in the absence of scientific evidence.

Developing countries need better access to each others' markets. When developing countries were locked into exporting only primary commodities they had relatively little potential for trade with each other. Now that their exports have diversified, there is massive scope for increased trade among them. Indeed, because developing countries tend to have tighter trade restrictions than developed countries, they have even more to gain from greater trade with each other than from greater trade with the developed countries. The model estimates that they would gain $27.6 billion per year by opening their own markets for manufactures and $31.4 billion by opening their own markets in agricultural produce.

Large global benefits from temporary movement of service providers

The current round of services negotiations at the WTO offers a valuable opportunity to liberalize the temporary movement of individual service suppliers. Many developing countries could then "export" the significant labor component of construction, distribution, environmental, transport, and other services. If the movement is temporary, then we can be fairly confident that both the host and home country will gain. For exporting countries, it is clear that both the financial and knowledge benefits would be greatest if service suppliers return home after a certain period abroad. And for importing countries, such temporary movement should create fewer social and political problems than immigration.

Negotiating a Development Round

Despite the potential gains from further trade liberalization, the effort at the Seattle ministerial meeting to launch a new round of trade liberalization was a disaster. Basically, rich and poor countries were pursuing different agendas. The recent report of the U.N. High-Level Panel on Financing for Development argues that:

> The Seattle WTO ministerial meeting failed to launch a new round, not because of the protests in the streets, but because the major trading powers lacked the political will to accommodate the interests of developing countries... In order for developing countries to have confidence in a new round, rich countries must deliver on commitments made in the past, such as accelerating the agricultural trade negotiations and phasing out quotas on textiles and clothing (p. 6).

If indeed the major obstacle to a "development round" was the lack of political will of developed countries, it might be imagined that this is because the developed countries would lose from liberalization. This is simply not the case. The model estimates that the developed countries would gain in absolute terms even more than developing countries from enhanced global market access. Developed countries would gain about $50 billion from improved access in the markets of developing countries and nearly $100 billion from improved access to each others' markets. The benefits from market access negotiations are addressed in more detail in the World Bank's *Global Economic Prospects 2002*.

In addition to the benefits from tariff reduction presented in table 2.1, developing countries could potentially gain from reductions in antidumping duties, safeguard measures, excessive standards barriers, and barriers to trade in services. The available estimates suggest that the benefits of liberalizing services are of the same order of magnitude as those for goods, and those from anti-dumping, safeguards, and standards are likely also of the same magnitude. A conservative estimate of the total impact of industrial country barriers on developing countries is likely to be more than $100 billion, rather than the $43 billion given in table 2.1.

Implementation concerns

Improved market access is not the only issue for a "development round". The implementation concerns of developing countries cover a number of issues, of which some of the more important are the slow pace of removal of quotas on textiles and clothing, anti-dumping measures in the industrial countries, and a desire by some countries to keep Trade-Related Investment Measures (TRIMs). In addition, there are concerns about the implementation of the TRIPs agreement, the Customs Valuation Agreement, and with the costs of meeting many product standards. These must be addressed before developing countries will feel comfortable engaging in a round, and many of them imply a need for significant reforms. We take them in turn.

Unfortunately, the rules on textiles and clothing were written in a way that allowed industrial countries to greatly delay the abolition of their quotas. Instead of specifying the progressive abolition of quotas, the rules specified the progressive integration of textiles and clothing under GATT disciplines. Industrial countries were allowed to choose the products to be integrated; almost without exception, they chose to begin by integrating the products in which developing countries do not have a comparative advantage. Developing countries that thought roughly half of their exports of textiles and clothing would be integrated by 2002 found that almost all would remain restricted until December 31, 2005—creating concerns about potential backsliding in the industrial countries.

The anti-dumping rules of the WTO make no economic sense and allow countries to restrict imports when there is no economic justification. Developing countries bear a disproportionate burden of these measures in both industrial country markets and other developing countries. While Japan is seriously burdened by anti-dumping actions, Finger, Ng, and Sonam (2000) show that some developing countries face 30 times as many anti-dumping actions per dollar of exports as does Japan. It is clear that some form of contingent protection is needed when countries find themselves politically unable to maintain an open stance, but more efficient and transparent safeguard systems that do not involve the abuses of anti-dumping can be developed (Finger 1998).

Many developing countries have expressed concern about requirements in the Uruguay Round agreement to phase out their trade-related investment measures. While some such measures may have an economic justification in countervailing the anti-export bias of the trade regime, most are merely an inefficient means of subsidizing multinational enterprises. This issue does highlight the problems associated with the traditional GATT approach of allowing time for implementation without respect to a country's stage of development.

A number of Uruguay Round agreements, such as those on TRIPs, customs valuation, and product standards, require developing countries to establish new institutions or to greatly strengthen existing ones. Further, some of these agreements effectively codify the established practices of the industrial countries, rather than seeking approaches to deal with these problems in the context of the developing countries. Finger and Schuler (2001) conclude that the Customs Valuation Agreement does not address the problems faced by developing countries and may cause serious loss of customs revenue under the conditions prevailing in many developing countries—unless a great deal is done to modernize and strengthen the customs service. But such investments in institutions are very expensive, and any such investment must be evaluated in the context of the country's overall development program.

The TRIPs agreement has raised many concerns about its implications for the cost of essential drugs. While there is widespread appreciation in developing countries of the need for some form of intellectual property protection in the emerging knowledge economy, there are concerns that current rules might price many patented drugs and other vital patented goods out of the reach of poor people in developing countries. This issue has been highlighted by a recent court case against the South African government for, among other things, allowing parallel imports of drugs in an attempt to lower prices. There is considerable flexibility in the current WTO rules to allow differential pricing of drugs, but some reforms may be needed to deal with the concerns of smaller developing countries that are unable to produce drugs themselves. If more fundamental reforms are considered, Jean Lanjouw (2001) has offered an interesting proposal for how the intellectual property rights for pharmaceuticals could be altered to ensure that poor countries have access to critical drugs at the marginal cost of production (box 2.1).

Box 2.1 Altering intellectual property rights over pharmaceuticals to benefit poor countries

JEAN LANJOUW (2001) PROPOSES AN INNOVATIVE way to amend the international system for Intellectual Property Rights (IPRs) for drugs that address global diseases. In her scheme, pharmaceutical innovators can choose to have IPRs in either rich country markets or poor country markets, but not both. So, in the case of the anti-viral drugs that fight HIV/AIDS, it would be in the interest of the pharmaceutical companies—who did the research and development primarily with rich country markets in mind—to choose patents for rich country markets. The technologies would then be freely available in developing countries, but producers there could not export cheap drugs back to the rich countries. Lanjouw's point is that this system would be a very minor disincentive to innovation because most of the potential rents are in rich country markets. As a result, poor countries would have access to cheap drugs but the incentives for innovation worldwide would still be strong. The nice thing about this proposal is that it would not discourage pharmaceutical companies from R&D on global diseases for which the main market is in developing countries. Where there is little demand in OECD markets for an innovation, then IPRs in developing countries can be an important incentive for firms (based anywhere) to research and develop products addressing the problem. Lanjouw's regime illustrates that IPRs are important to stimulate innovation and that it is in the interests of developing countries to protect rights that will lead to more innovation on their problems. On the other hand, there is nothing in it for developing countries to protect IPRs on treatments for AIDS or cancers that are common in rich countries, because that research will go ahead anyway, based on returns in OECD markets.

Participation concerns

If a new round is to be a true "development round", it must take into account the greatly changed nature of the trade agenda following the Uruguay Round and its implications for the participation of civil society. Before the Uruguay Round, GATT negotiations tended to be over relatively arcane issues of tariff policy. Typically, these negotiations were conducted by negotiators and bureaucrats without much discussion of the issues in civil society. This has all changed with the expansion of the numbers of countries participating in the negotiations and the deepening of the trade agenda to include behind-the-border issues such as regulation of trade in services and IPRs.

The broadening of participation by developing countries has created a participation problem for the smaller developing countries that remains serious. Even for those smaller developing countries that have a permanent mission in Geneva, the diversity and complexity of the issues makes it impossible to participate effectively on more than a small range of issues. Almost half the least developed countries are not even represented in Geneva, making it impossible for them to participate fully.

Related to the participation problem is an "ownership" problem that results when outcomes of negotiations have not been sufficiently discussed and debated within countries for the countries to feel a commitment to implement them fully. Cooperation between researchers in developing countries through networks such as the African Economic Research Consortium and the Latin American Trade Network is strengthening the analytical basis for informed debate on the issues, but more is needed to build the necessary basis for wider understanding.

Given the substantial investments involved, developing countries need to formulate their trade policy objectives within their overall development programs. Much greater cooperation between ministries within developing countries, and between development agencies and the WTO at the international level, is needed. The Integrated Framework for Technical Assistance to the Least Developed Countries is an initial attempt to integrate trade and development partners in support of the least developed countries, and may provide a prototype for deepening such cooperation in the future.

A great deal also needs to be done to build the domestic institutions to support a "development round". For example, taking advantage of product standards requires institutions to conduct testing and certify the results. Administering TRIPs requires the development of patent offices and related institutions. Development of these institutions is costly and time consuming, unlike traditional tariff cutting, and requires a great deal of support from development partners.

Keeping at bay the new protectionist agenda

There are various proposals to introduce new issues into negotiations. These proposals rightly generate concern among developing countries. In particular, they oppose the notion of using trade sanctions to impose labor and environmental standards. There is a real danger that these would turn into new protectionist tools. Improving labor standards and working conditions is at the heart of the development process and requires a legal framework and programs of the type discussed in Chapter 3 to be developed and expanded. Our assessment is that measures to support these positive programs offer a great deal more potential for improving labor standards than the use of punitive sanctions—especially when the risk of protectionist capture of labor standards is taken into account.

The interaction between environmental and trade measures is a vital issue, and one where markets frequently fail. There is a strong case for international cooperation on these issues, particularly where they involve international spillovers. However, in most cases, they are best dealt with in international forums established for the purpose, or a potential multilateral environmental agency, rather than the WTO, whose focus is on trade reform. These issues are discussed in more depth in Chapter 4.

Should there be global rules on investment? There are potentially substantial gains from the negotiation of international rules on investment. Such rules might, for instance, address the subsidies paid to attract investors. Unbridled competition for investment frequently results in incentives that are excessively generous, and creates an environment in which the deepest pockets—almost by definition not those of developing countries—are successful in attracting investment. They might also help developing countries attract investment by reducing the perception of risk in developing countries, and hence lower the cost of attracting investment. Such negotiations might be pursued either under the rubric of a special agreement on investment, or by building on the framework developed under GATS for trade in services undertaken by establishment within a market (Mode 3 of GATS). Whatever the approach, it is vitally important that the issue be approached in a transparent way, with maximum participation, and on the basis of a common understanding of the issues. Perhaps the primary lesson of the abortive Multilateral Agreement on Investment (MAI) negotiations at the OECD is that negotiations on such issues require widespread participation and discussion.

Should there be global rules on competition? Competition policy issues also warrant careful consideration. Smaller developing countries, with their smaller markets, are more vulnerable to a lack of competition than the rich countries. While many of these problems are domestic, and amenable to purely domestic policy solutions, others are beyond the scope of domestic reforms. In shipping, for example, Fink, Mattoo, and Neagu (2001) estimate that shipping costs are inflated by an average of 25 percent by the anti-competitive practices of international liner shipping firms. While the larger rich countries could deal with this problem unilaterally, smaller developing countries are not likely to be able to do so, and Fink, Mattoo, and Neagu recommend that stronger disciplines on restrictive business practices be developed in the current round of services trade negotiations at the WTO. However, care must be taken that competition law reflects national concerns, priorities, and institutional capacities (World Bank forthcoming).

Regional blocs

A final concern involves regional trade blocs. The regional approach to international engagement frequently appears attractive for two reasons: because it provides preferential access to partner markets, and because it may be easier to make progress with a small number of partners than with the 140 members of the WTO. These perceptions, and the increasing length of multilateral negotiations, have contributed to the dramatic increase in the number of regional trade agreements during recent years (figure 2.2). However, the advantages of South-South trade blocs are typically much less substantial than they might at first appear. They risk divisive redistributions without generating many overall gains. The companion report, *Trade Blocs* (World Bank 2000b), discusses this in detail.

Policies for capital flows to developing countries

AS DISCUSSED IN CHAPTER 1, CAPITAL FLOWS TO DEVELOPING countries have increased massively during third wave globalization, and have shifted from aid, which actually declined during

Figure 2.2 World Trade Organization notifications of regional integration agreements

Number of agreements

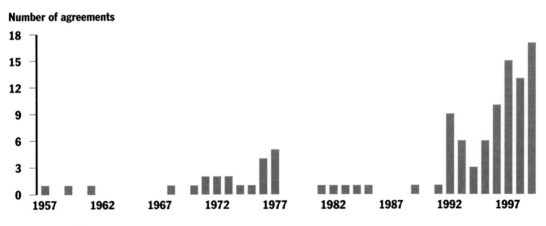

Source: WTO data.

the 1990s, to private capital. This change has also affected the destination of capital flows. Private capital goes predominantly to large and middle-income globalizing economies. This makes targeting aid flows more critical. We first discuss how aid can be better targeted in order to complement private flows. The largest component of private flows has been FDI. We defer discussion of this until Chapter 3, where we focus on the domestic investment climate. Financial flows, though smaller, have been more controversial and problematic. We consider them later in this section.

Aid flows

Low-income countries that reform have trouble attracting investment. Here aid can play a helpful complementary role in assisting countries that reform their policies in the hope of becoming new globalizers. Aid reinforces the favorable effect of good policies on investment. Thus, one of the reasons why aid raises growth in good policy environments is that it attracts investment. Conversely, Burnside and Dollar (2000) show that large volumes of aid going into a poor policy environment produce little in the way of measurable growth, poverty reduction, or improvements in social indicators.

The conclusion to be drawn is that reallocating aid could increase poverty reduction. Aid should be shifted toward the low-income reformers and away from both middle-income countries that are able to attract private flows and countries with such poor policies that aid is unlikely to be effective. While this may seem like commonsense advice, as recently as 1996 the world was not doing it (Collier and Dollar forthcoming a). The allocation of aid had little relationship to poverty and no relationship to the quality of economic institutions and policies. The authors estimate that the impact of aid on poverty reduction could be roughly doubled by better allocation toward poor countries and ones with reasonably sound policies. In the past five years there has been some significant improvement in the use of aid. The concessional resources managed by the World Bank go to low-income countries and, among these countries, are allocated toward ones with good economic governance. Some major bilateral donors have moved in the same direction. Together with this has come a shift away from detailed conditionality in which donor agencies try to dictate every aspect of policy—an approach that generally did not work.

Collier and Dollar (forthcoming b) apply this model of assistance to poverty reduction in Africa. They conclude that a better allocation of donor assistance could significantly increase poverty reduction there. Most importantly, the combination of African policy reform and generous, well-targeted aid could make a substantial dent in poverty. Their analysis highlights the need for greater volumes of aid, especially if large countries in Africa such as Ethiopia and Nigeria follow through on policy reform.

The targeting of aid to low-income countries with good policies will help currently marginalized countries that aim to participate more in the global economy. Aid can also be helpful to those countries that, for whatever reason, stay marginalized. But in view of the past record it must be carefully thought through.

One of the major problems for the many marginalized countries that are heavily dependent upon primary commodity exports is their exposure to severe negative terms of trade shocks. New research finds that aid would be highly effective in mitigating the growth-reducing effects of shocks if it was increased at such times (Collier and Dehn 2001). Again, while this seems a commonsense use of aid, in practice aid flows have not responded promptly to adverse terms-of-trade shocks. Streamlining the efficiency of aid delivery (eliminating tied aid and numerous conditionalities) would make it easier for donors to respond flexibly to shocks.

Aid can also be targeted to specific problems affecting marginalized areas. For example, much more could be done to fund research into treatment or prevention of malaria, tuberculosis, and AIDS. The United Nations has called on industrial countries to provide $10 billion per year to fight health problems of poor countries, but so far they have pledged only $1.3 billion. While rich country incomes have grown well during this third wave of globalization, their foreign aid has declined to the historically low level of 0.2 percent of national income.

Another important aid issue is debt relief. Many of the marginalized countries are burdened with heavy external debts. The HIPC initiative is aimed at relieving this debt burden. However, it is important that debt relief represent new resources from the rich countries and not come out of existing aid. In general, HIPC initiative countries receive large gross flows of aid, so that even after servicing their debts they have significant net inflows of official aid. If their debts are forgiven but the flow of aid is reduced by a commensurate amount, then nothing real will have happened. It is the combination of debt relief and continued high gross flows of aid that would actually give these countries more resources for education, health, and other services.

Private financial flows

Third wave globalization has also been characterized by much greater involvement of developing countries in international financial flows. As Mundell (2000) argues, the 1970s witnessed the beginning of a new era in the international financial system. The oil shock provided international banks with fresh funds to invest in developing countries. Initially, these funds were used mainly to finance public debt in the form of syndicated loans. With the breakup of the Bretton Woods system of fixed exchange rates, countries were able to open up to greater capital mobility while keeping autonomy over their monetary policies.

The globalizing developing countries have gradually lifted their restrictions on capital account (figure 2.3). However, they have been partially re-introduced in the wake of crises, notably the Asian crisis of 1997.

As a result of these policy changes and technological advance, net private financial flows to developing economies have increased sharply since the 1970s. This greater supply of capital is a potential benefit of financial globalization. However, while financial globalization can bring benefits—especially for large and middle-income countries—it has also been associated in recent years with financial crises that carry devastating costs. Because of these crises, there is a perception that financially open countries experience more volatility. Surprisingly, the evidence suggests that *in the long run* volatility tends to decrease following liberalization and

Figure 2.3 Restrictions on capital account

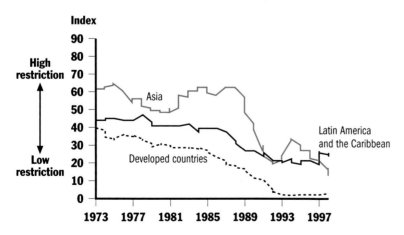

Note: The data cover selected countries from the specified region.
Source: Schmukler and Zoido-Lobatón (2001).

integration with world markets, probably owing to diversification of asset portfolios and healthier development of the financial sector. However, the fact that open economies are less volatile in the long run is of little solace if the process of opening up temporarily increases the risk of a crisis. As a result, we would like to emphasize the distinction that *being open* financially is associated with greater stability, whereas *becoming open* financially is often associated with financial and exchange rate crises. Developing countries such as China and India that are relatively closed on their capital account should therefore approach liberalization very carefully.

There is considerable debate as to whether financial crises are a greater problem today than in the past. Bordo, Eichengreen, Klingebiel, and Martinez-Peria (2001) study the frequency, duration, and impact on economic output of crises during the past 120 years. They compare the crises of third wave globalization with the two previous waves and with the retreat of the inter-war years. They conclude that crises are more frequent today than during the previous waves of globalization and are comparable to the inter-war years. There is little evidence that crises have grown longer or output losses have become larger. Bordo, Eichengreen, and Irwin (1999) compare today's wave of globalization with that of a century ago, taking into account the much greater degree of integration in today's global economy. They conclude it is surprising that financial instability is not worse. The authors conclude that the diminished risk of financial crisis can be attributed to the development of institutional innovations at both a global level and a local level (such as better accounting standards and contract enforcement).

What causes these crises and what can be done to mitigate the risks? The vast literature on financial crises stresses the importance of domestic factors as one key determinant of crises. Caprio and Klingebiel (1997), for example, stress the importance of both macroeconomic and microeconomic policies in determining banking crises. Similarly, Burnside, Eichenbaum, and Rebelo (forthcoming) argue that crises are determined not only by typical macroeconomic indicators such as actual deficits, but by other factors that generate large prospective deficits. A country's fiscal situation may look good on the surface, but a prospective deficit associated with implicit bailout guarantees to failing banks can help generate a crisis. In the countries affected by the Asian crisis, governments were actually running surpluses or negligible deficits, but had large implicit liabilities resulting from guarantees of deteriorating financial systems.

Thus, when countries first liberalize their financial sector, volatility and crises are more likely to arise if they have vulnerable fundamentals. Kaminsky and Schmukler (2001b) show that the process of opening up leads to a more extreme cycle in financial markets. In the typical stock market cycle of an open developing country, stock prices double during the 18 months before the cycle peaks, and then fall 20 percent over the first six months of the downturn (figure 2.4). For the first cycle within three years of financial liberalization, however, stock prices triple and then drop by 50 percent over the first six months of the downturn. Thus, a key question for developing countries is whether they have the robust financial institutions to manage this temporary volatility. If not, a serious crisis can ensue.

Second, crises can also be generated by errors in international financial markets. Financial markets can generate bubbles, irrational behavior, herding behavior, speculative attacks, and crashes. These can lead to crises even in countries with sound fundamentals. For example, if investors believe that the exchange rate is unsustainable they might speculate against the currency, which can lead to a self-fulfilling balance-of-payments crisis regardless of market fundamentals (Obstfeld 1986). Errors can also undermine fundamentals. For example, moral hazard can lead to over-borrowing when economies are liberalized and there are

Figure 2.4   Liberalizing temporarily amplifies the boom-bust cycle

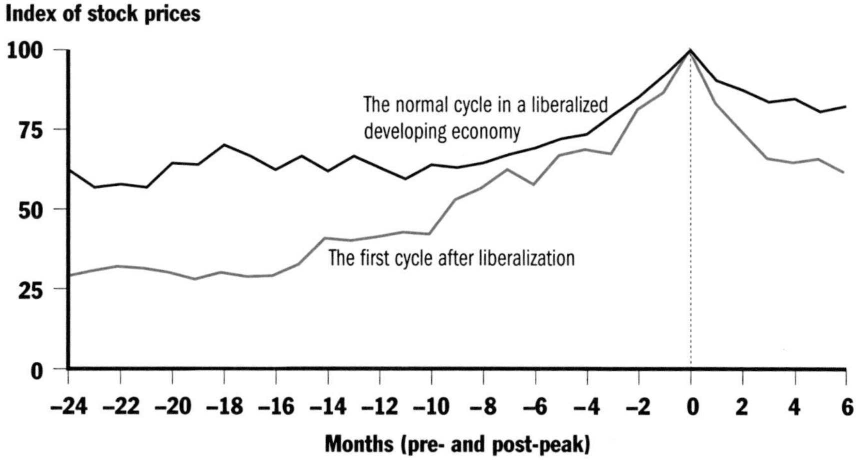

Index of stock prices

Months (pre- and post-peak)

Source: Kaminsky and Schmukler (2001b).

implicit government guarantees, increasing the likelihood of crises, as argued in McKinnon and Pill (1997).

Third, globalization can lead to crises due to the importance of external factors, even in countries with sound fundamentals and even in the absence of errors in international capital markets. If a country becomes dependent on foreign capital, sudden shifts in foreign capital flows can create financing difficulties and economic downturns. These shifts do not necessarily depend on a country's fundamentals. Calvo, Leiderman, and Reinhart (1996) argue that external factors are important determinants of capital flows to developing countries. In particular, they find that world interest rates were a significant determinant of capital inflows into Asia and Latin America during the 1990s. Frankel and Rose (1996) highlight the role that foreign interest rates play in determining the likelihood of financial crises in developing countries.

Contagion—the spreading of crisis from one country to another—can also be due to herding behavior. The magnitudes of recent swings in exchange rates and stock prices across countries seem to be beyond those predicted by any fundamental linkages. Shocks were indeed transmitted to economies where fundamental linkages are not present or strong, due to shifts in expectations. Herding leads investors to panic and flee countries that do not necessarily share fundamental linkages. The issue of herding behavior is one of multiple equilibria. If markets regard a country's state to be good, then large capital inflows can take place. If markets judge the country as being in a bad state, then rapid capital outflows and a crisis can occur. In a world of "multiple" equilibria, external shocks can quickly force the economy to shift from a "good" to a "bad" equilibrium. When investors suddenly become concerned about emerging markets for any reason, Wall Street reacts and European markets follow. When investors observe a crisis in Thailand, they react by thinking about a potential crisis in Indonesia and Malaysia, and a crisis indeed takes place. Both industrial and developing country markets are subject to these panics. Because investors know little about developing countries, they are probably more prone to herding behavior in these markets. Uninformed investors are the ones that find market changes more informative.

How can countries insulate themselves from these financial crises? We will emphasize four options that are not mutually exclusive: exchange rate management, supervision and regulation of the financial system, capital controls, and international crisis management.

The choice of exchange rate regime (floating, fixed, or somewhere in between) is a recurring question in international monetary economics.

It has become more important with the increasing integration of financial markets. All countries face the "impossible trinity"—that a country must choose two of the following three policies: fixed exchange rate, autonomous monetary policy, and free capital mobility. Pursuing all three leads to inconsistencies such that one of the three will be abandoned. After the crises of the 1990s it has become increasingly clear that countries with open capital accounts are being pushed toward "corner solutions"—either firmly fixing their exchange rate or following a flexible regime without pre-commitments. Which solution is best depends on the specific country and its circumstances.

By fixing the exchange rate, countries reduce transaction costs and exchange rate risk that can discourage trade and investment. At the same time, a fixed exchange rate has been used as a credible nominal anchor for monetary policy. On the other hand, a flexible exchange rate allows a country to pursue independent monetary policy responding to shocks through changes in the exchange rate and interest rate, to avoid going into recession. Under the combination of fixed exchange rates and complete integration of financial markets, monetary policy becomes powerless. Any fluctuations in the currency or currencies to which the country fixes its exchange rate will affect the domestic currency. Under a fixed exchange rate regime, other variables must do the adjustment.

Whether countries go with fixed or flexible rates, it is important to be firm about the choice if the capital account is open. The worst crises have occurred in countries that have managed their exchange rates to be relatively stable without a firm commitment to the fixed rate. In Thailand, for example, the long stability of the baht against the dollar encouraged firms and households to borrow in dollars to make domestic fixed investments—a highly risky situation susceptible to speculative attack.

A second important area for action is government regulation and supervision of the financial system. It is important to ensure that the financial sector is managing risk well. Government regulation and supervision should encourage financial institutions to avoid large mismatches between assets and liabilities, such as unhedged foreign exchange borrowings invested in non-tradable sectors and short-term assets used to finance long-term investments. These risky practices leave banks vulnerable to exchange rate depreciations and interest rate surges. Also, the regulation and supervision should ensure that banks are sufficiently capitalized with appropriate loan classification and adequate loan loss provisions. Transparency for investors and depositors through mandatory public disclosure of audited financial statements will help to enforce market discipline. The removal of explicit or implicit government guarantees and sharing risk with investors will decrease the potential for moral hazard. *Finance for Growth* (World Bank 2001a) discusses in more detail the regulation of the financial sector in an integrated economy.

The recent experiences with crises and contagion highlight the importance of adequate risk management. Kawai, Newfarmer, and Schmukler (2001) argue that one of the more important lessons of the East Asian crisis is that highly leveraged and vulnerable corporate sectors were a key determinant of the depth of the crisis. Currency devaluations suddenly inflated the size of external debt (measured in terms of the domestic currency) and debt service obligations, thereby driving the domestic corporations into financial distress. High interest rates also sharply increased the corporations' domestic debt service obligations. These vulnerabilities affected the banks with exposures to the corporations. Krugman (1999) argues that company balance sheet problems may have a role in causing financial crises. Currency crises lead to an increase in foreign-denominated debt, which combined with declining sales and higher interest rates weakens the corporate sector and, in turn, the financial system.

Can financial liberalization take place without the appropriate risk management in place? This question leads to the issue of sequencing of liberalization. Having a robust financial sector is key for a successful globalization. But not all the conditions need to be in place before governments start to open up the financial sector. In particular, international financial services can help to strengthen the financial system so that it is better placed to integrate with world financial markets. It is difficult to achieve a very robust financial system while the country remains closed to foreign financial institutions.

A third policy issue concerns capital controls, which can be designed to reduce the probability or mitigate the effects of sudden shifts in foreign capital. Various proposals suggest that international capital flows should be restricted in very particular and judicious ways. Following the classification in Frankel (1999), the main proposals can be divided into several categories: (1) controls on outflows, which restrict investors to move capital outside the country; (2) controls on aggregate inflows, which are intended to keep capital from flowing into the country rather than restricting the exit of capital once it is in the country; (3) controls on short-term inflows, as were introduced in Chile, to avoid the build up of short-term debt; and (4) controls on foreign exchange transactions, or the so-called Tobin tax, aimed at imposing a small uniform tax on all foreign exchange transactions, regardless of their nature.

There is a very large literature on the effects of capital controls. On the whole, it finds mixed results. Probably the country whose capital controls have received the most attention is Chile, which imposed capital controls on short-term inflows through unremunerated reserve requirements. Chile was widely studied because it systematically put limits to capital flows in both episodes of international capital inflows to emerging markets (1978–81 and 1990–96). The evidence from studies including De Gregorio, Edwards, and Valdes (1998); Edwards (1999); Gallego, Hernández, and Schmidt-Hebbel (1999); and Soto (1997) suggests that controls on inflows introduce a wedge between domestic and foreign returns and allowed Chile's central bank to undertake a more independent monetary policy. This finding holds only when external shocks were small. Controls were not effective in preventing spillovers from very large shocks, such as the ones observed in the midst of the Asian crisis in 1997.

The experience with capital account controls in Asia has also been analyzed in various studies. The evidence for this region is also mixed. Reisen and Yeches (1993) examine the degree of monetary independence in Korea and Taiwan, China and find that capital mobility remained roughly constant in the 1980s in the presence of capital controls. However, these studies are concerned mostly with the degree of capital mobility in episodes of financial repression and do not compare these estimates with those in periods of financial liberalization. Analyzing the more recent experience in Malaysia, Kaplan and Rodrik (2001) argue that the Malaysian controls were able to segment financial markets and provided room for monetary and financial policies, allowing a speedier recovery from the crisis. They compare the recovery to what would have been possible with a more traditional response to the crisis. China is another interesting case, which apparently succeeded in remaining isolated from the recent crises although it could not avoid experiencing recent capital outflows.

The number of multicountry studies is much more limited due to the lack of comparable data on capital control measures across countries. Montiel and Reinhart (1999) construct a database for capital account restrictions of 15 emerging economies during the 1990s to study the effect of restrictions to capital inflows. They find that controls appear to alter the composition of capital flows in the direction usually intended by these measures, reducing the share of short-term and portfolio flows while increasing that of FDI. Another cross-country study with a new measure of capital account restrictions is that of Kaminsky and Schmukler (2001a), who find that controls work at best temporarily, with the effects diminishing over time.

Finally, as economies become more integrated, governments have fewer policy instruments and must rely more on international financial coordination. For example, bank regulation and supervision by one government is more difficult when liabilities and prices are denominated in foreign currency and when the banking sector is part of an international banking system. Also, in the midst of contagious crises, governments tend to lack sufficient resources to stop a currency attack and an individual government can do little to stop crises that originated in foreign countries. In these cases, international financial coordination can help individual governments achieve their goals.

Coordination is possible on a range of policies. One of the most important is the timely mobilization of external liquidity of sufficient magnitude to reverse market expectations in a context of sound policies. That liquidity usually comes from the international financial institutions, especially the International Monetary Fund (IMF). Given the magnitude of capital flows and the clustering of crises, isolated actions of individual governments or institutions are not sufficient to gain the required confidence. A coordinated action among governments and the international financial institutions is necessary to overcome crises and contagion, at both regional and global levels. To minimize potential moral hazard, it is necessary to involve the private sector so that private international investors share in the costs as penalty for excessive risk taking.

There is much that the world can do to improve the international financial architecture to prevent and manage financial crises in a systematic way. Current initiatives include setting international standards for transparency and dissemination of information, bank supervision and regulation, disclosure in securities markets, accounting and auditing rules, bankruptcy procedures, and corporate governance. New initiatives also include private sector involvement in financing packages to complement IMF resources and discourage moral hazard that could be associated with bailouts.

Policies toward migration

MIGRATION CAN POTENTIALLY DO MUCH TO HELP REGIONS that do not now benefit greatly from globalization. However, while economic pressures for migration are strong and growing, legal migration is highly restricted. Compared to 100 years ago, the world is much less globalized when it comes to labor flows.

Let us look at the migration policies of a number of OECD countries, starting with the largest economy, the United States. The United States had an extremely open policy in the late 19th and early 20th centuries, and large flows of immigrants, primarily from Europe. As a vast country with a lot of room to absorb newcomers, the United States also attracted capital flows throughout much of this period, which meant that high levels of migration went hand-in-hand with high and rising wages. However, by the time of the First World War and the early years afterwards, immigration had become a controversial subject in the United States. There was political mobilization against immigrants and a sharp shift in U.S. policy. The change in policy can be seen clearly in the sudden decline in the number of immigrants entering the country (figure 2.5).

After several decades of relatively restrictive migration, policies began to ease in the 1970s and especially the 1980s and led to an expanding volume of immigration. In contrast to the largely European immigration of the 1870–1910 wave, contemporary immigration into the United States comes largely from Latin America and Asia. As a result, the foreign population comprised 10 percent of the U.S. population in 1998 and a somewhat larger share of the labor force (reflecting the fact that most migrants move in order to work). If one adds in the estimated 5 million undocumented workers in the Unites States, then migrants make up about 12 percent of the U.S. population.

U.S. immigration policies are quite complex. Some migrants are allowed in to fill specific labor needs. Some of these shortages in the U.S.

Figure 2.5   Immigrants to the United States by sending region, 1820–1998

Millions

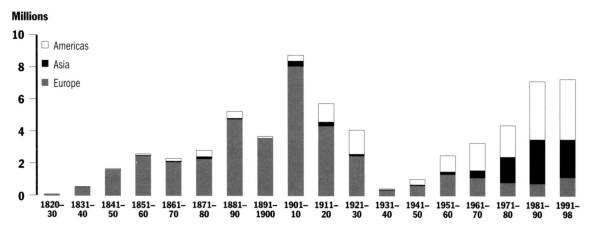

Source: Immigration and Naturalization Service (1998).

economy are in high-tech fields, leading to selective immigration of highly skilled engineers and medical professionals. But other shortages are in low-skilled areas (73 percent of all workers employed in crop production are immigrants), allowing immigration of unskilled workers from developing countries. Finally, U.S. law puts considerable weight on family connections. Now that there are sizeable numbers of Latin American and Asian emigrants who have settled in the United States, the family connections lead to immigration of a diverse group of people. The average immigrant into the country is less skilled than the average American, so that on balance migration brings the level of skills in the United States closer to the world average.

Migration is a controversial topic in rich countries, for both economic and social reasons. On the economic side, theory suggests that a large inflow of low-skilled workers from the South would put downward pressure on wages for those native workers without a high degree of education. A number of studies of individual U.S. cities find very small estimated effects of immigration on wages, but these studies are problematic because they treat the city as a closed economy that has an exogenous inflow of migrants. There is in fact a lot of city-to-city movement of Americans, which would render these estimates suspect. For example, if migrants are attracted to a particular location because of family connections and native workers then move away to other locations in response to downward pressure on wages, one would find similar wage trends in cities receiving immigrants and cities not receiving immigrants, but it would be incorrect to infer that immigration has no effect on wages.

Borjas, Freeman, and Katz (1997) correct for this problem by looking at the nationwide effects of immigration. Their first finding of interest is that overall immigration increased the unskilled labor supply by 21 percent and the skilled labor supply by 4 percent between 1975 and 1995. So, despite some bias in U.S. law toward high-tech workers, the overall weight of U.S. immigration is tilted clearly toward unskilled workers. The second finding of interest is that the estimated effect of these labor supply changes was to decrease the relative wages of unskilled workers by 5 percent. That may not sound like a large number, but it was 44 percent of the widening wage gap between skilled and unskilled workers. The evidence is consistent with the view that technological change has shifted the relative demand for labor toward higher-skilled workers, so that even without immigration there would have been a decline in the relative earnings of unskilled workers. The inflow of a large number of unskilled migrants at the same time pushed the relative wage down further and exacerbated mounting inequality.

From this, it is easy to see why immigration is controversial economically. An inflow of unskilled workers from the South will benefit highly skilled workers in the North. Their jobs are not threatened by these immigrants, and the presence of immigrants will lower prices for many things that the skilled workers consume (including food, restaurant and hotel services, and personal services—all areas of the economy in which unskilled workers tend to congregate). On the other hand, the same inflow will reduce real wages of unskilled northern workers from what they would be otherwise.

Immigration policies of OECD countries toward workers from developing countries vary substantially. One reflection of this is the variation in the share of legal immigrants from developing countries in OECD populations. For the G-7 countries, the share varies from about 10 percent in Canada to 8 percent in the United States, 6 percent in Germany, 3 percent in France, and 2 percent or less in the United Kingdom, Italy, and Japan (figure 2.6). In most of the rich countries, policies explicitly discriminate in favor of educated immigrants, encouraging so-called "brain drain" from the South. Recent Japanese economic plans, for example, note the policy of readily accepting foreigners possessing technological expertise but discouraging immigration of

Figure 2.6 Developing country migrants relative to total population in the G-7 countries, 1998

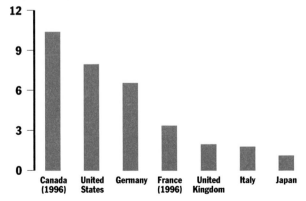

Migrants as percent of total population

Source: OECD (various years).

low-skilled workers. European policies generally aim to address labor shortages in high-tech and service industries.

Because immigration is very attractive economically and also highly restricted, there is naturally growing illegal immigration and trafficking in human beings. For the United States, there is an estimated net inflow of about 300,000 undocumented workers per year. But that figure is for the net increase in the stock of undocumented workers. Many more cross temporarily into the United States. In 1999 U.S. authorities apprehended 1.5 million illegal immigrants along the Mexican border. The great majority sent back to Mexico attempt to cross again within 24 hours.

Illegal migration into the EU has soared ten-fold in the 1990s, from an estimated 50,000 per year in 1993 to half a million in 1999 (figure 2.7). This illegal trade in people has become big business, with estimated revenues of $10–12 billion per year. Smugglers charge as little as $500 for a short hop across a single border (for example, Morocco to Spain). The price for a complex journey—for example, from East Asia to Western Europe—can go as high as $70,000.

Illegal immigrants are vulnerable to exploitation. Bolivians trying to enter Argentina, for example, must carry at least $1,500 (an attempt to distinguish tourists from undocumented workers). Not surprisingly, a new market has sprung up in which Bolivian migrants can borrow the $1,500 for one hour to cross the border—for a fee of 10 percent (Stalker 2000).

Figure 2.7 Illegal migration into the European Union, 1993–99

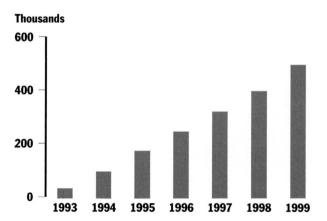

Source: International Center for Migration Policy Development data.

The pressures for migration of unskilled workers will become even stronger because of demographic factors. Each year, 83 million people are added to world population, 82 million of them in the developing world. Population pressures affect wages and hence migration, in the intuitive direction. Higher rates of population growth, other things equal, are associated with more out-migration.

Most of the increase in the working-age population in the next 15 years will occur in South Asia and Sub-Saharan Africa, the two regions in which poverty is currently concentrated (figure 2.8). At the same time, the working-age population in Western Europe and Japan will decline, given current birth rates and immigration policies. In Japan and the EU, the ratio of workers to retirees will decline from five to one today to three to one in 2015, without greater migration, putting a strain on social security systems. Potentially, there is mutual

Figure 2.8   Regional population by age group, 2000 and 2015

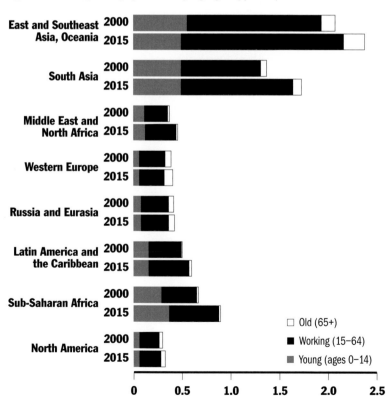

Source: U.S. Bureau of the Census data.

economic benefit in combining the capital and technology of the OECD economies with labor from developing countries. To some extent that can occur through flows of capital and production to developing countries. But we have emphasized above geographic factors that make it unlikely that capital flows and trade will eliminate the economic rationale for migration. Too many locations in the developing world have poor institutions and infrastructure that will not attract production, plus some of the existing production networks in the industrial countries are too deeply rooted to move (for example, Silicon Valley and its links to nearby universities). Institutional and policy reform and infrastructure investments in lagging developing countries could address the former concern and reduce, though not eliminate, economic pressures for migration.

Migration is the most under-researched of the global flows. As a result, we want to be cautious about drawing conclusions about the effect of migration. But it seems that out-migration can benefit developing countries, especially if migration policies stopped discriminating in favor of highly skilled workers, leading to the "brain drain" effect. Suppose that there were more freedom for both unskilled and skilled workers to migrate from South to North. The outflow of unskilled migrants would benefit sending countries by raising wages for those who remain behind and by generating a flow of remittances. The outflow of more skilled workers would also generate remittances and is likely to have spillover effects on trade and investment between sending and receiving countries. In the rich countries, this migration will reduce wages of unskilled workers from what they would be otherwise. But keep in mind that the demographic trends in rich countries will lead to rising relative wages for unskilled labor in the absence of more migration. Thus, there is good potential for increased flows of unskilled workers to the rich countries in an environment of stable relative wages.

Summary of recommendations

I T IS IMPORTANT TO LAUNCH A NEW ROUND OF TRADE negotiations to maintain the momentum of global economic integration. Developing countries would benefit a lot from decreased protection in the rich world and from reducing their import tariffs and non-tariff barriers against each other. A "development round" of trade negotiations should focus on market access. Poor countries have a good argument that labor and environmental standards cannot be improved through trade sanctions. More generally, developing countries should be given more scope and freedom to develop institutions that work for them, and trade agreements should refrain from imposing a single institutional model.

Concerning the international financial architecture, the frequency and depth of international financial crises can be reduced through better international coordination concerning transparency and information disclosure and crisis management. We support efforts to involve the private sector in crisis workouts to ensure that private lenders bear some of the cost of crises and so that private lenders have good incentives to avoid excessively risky lending. At the same time, international efforts, led by the IMF, to mobilize liquidity for countries with sound policies facing short-run shocks or contagion are critical for the smooth operation of the international financial system. Developing countries can do a lot to reduce the risks of crisis through good exchange rate management and supervision and regulation of the financial system. We support the move by many countries to use the international market for financial and accounting services to help strengthen domestic financial infrastructure. Foreign aid is critical as a financial flow to the poorest countries. Rich countries should increase their aid and target it to low-income countries with sound policies and to problems of poor areas such as health challenges, connectivity, and agricultural technologies.

Migration will also have to be part of the solution for the large number of people living in poor locations. Within large countries (China, India) or continents such as Africa, there will be growing pressure for people to move from poor rural areas to towns and cities. There is room in the world economy for more manufacturing/service agglomerations, and these are likely to appear along coasts or major rivers, provided that there is a good investment climate to attract production. There will also be mounting pressures for migration from south to north, especially of unskilled workers. Rich countries should avoid immigration policies that focus exclusively on "brain drain" migration of highly skilled workers from south to north. Such policy will continue to drive unskilled workers into illegal migration, which has increased dramatically in the 1990s. With the aging of populations in rich countries and the surge in population in the areas where poverty is currently concentrated (South Asia and Africa), more freedom for unskilled workers to migrate to the north could be mutually beneficial.

Note

1.   That is, to enter into a commitment not to increase their tariffs above a specified level recorded in a schedule of concessions at the WTO.

CHAPTER THREE

Strengthening Domestic Institutions and Policies

GOOD POLICY IS ABOUT IDENTIFYING AND supporting the driving forces for poverty reduction, while at the same time identifying and meeting the risks. Those developing countries that are successfully integrating with the global economy are doing so not just because of relatively open trade and investment policies, but also because of effective policies and institutions in other areas. Whether closed or open, developing economies need such policies and institutions. In this chapter we consider the investment climate for firms, and labor market and social protection policies for workers. These will affect the extent to which a developing economy integrates with the world and the benefits it receives from this integration.

The next section looks at micro evidence about how openness to foreign trade and investment affects firms. Better collection of data from firms in developing countries has given rise to a burgeoning literature that studies these firm-level effects of openness. In particular, we document four stylized facts about economies that are relatively open to foreign trade and investment. First, open economies tend to have more competition and firm turnover ("churning"). Liberalization leads to the exit of many firms, and to higher entry rates as well. Second, the presence of imports leads to a more competitive market and lower price-cost mark-ups. Third, there is some evidence of technology spillovers from foreign trade and investment raising productivity of domestic firms. Fourth, there can be learning and threshold effects of exporting that create a better environment for productivity growth.

Individual cases and firm-level studies reveal that developing country firms can be competitive. However, firms are often hampered by a poor investment climate—inefficient regulation, corruption, infrastructure weaknesses, and poor financial services. In the second section we look at the investment climate. A recent study of India concludes that it is possible to measure the quality of the investment climate through firm surveys. With the same trade and macro policies (which are set at the national level), Indian states are getting widely different results from liberalization. "Good climate" states have more efficient regulation and better infrastructure, while "poor climate" states lag behind. Not surprisingly, the good climate states are getting more foreign investment and more domestic investment. If effective institutions are needed to get strong benefits from openness, should countries wait until they have such institutions to open up? Not necessarily. One of the reasons why liberalization of trade in services is so important is that developing countries can use this market to improve the investment climate: allowing foreign firms to provide financial services, telecommunications, and power can be a good strategy for strengthening the investment climate. A final issue we take up is targeted efforts to attract foreign investment. In the context of a good investment climate targeted efforts can work by overcoming the coordination problem—getting many investors to come to the same place at the same time. However, governments often try to attract investment through subsidies and tax holidays to compensate for defects in the investment climate. Such an approach is usually unsuccessful and also discriminates against domestic firms. Deficiencies are better remedied than offset by subsidies. The really successful cases—Taiwan, China is a good example—have created an environment of good governance and good infrastructure in which both foreign and domestic firms can be competitive.

Together with greater "churning" of firms comes higher labor market turnover, one of the most controversial aspects of global economic integration and the topic of the following section. In the long run integrating with the world economy benefits workers. The growth of wages in the more globalized developing countries identified in Chapter 1 has been far higher than in the rich countries or in the less globalized countries. But that average result disguises the fact that some workers are likely to lose rents that they were sharing from import protection and may suffer permanent income loss. Further, the short-run effects of opening can be quite different from the longer-run effects. In the short run the real wages of formal sector workers are reduced by trade openness and increased by direct foreign investment. Thus, in an economy that liberalizes trade and gets little foreign investment (either because the investment climate is weak or simply because there is a lagged response from investors), opening up can lead to temporary declines in formal sector wages. Also, openness seems to increase the skill premium (the higher wage that educated workers receive). Finally, there can be a mismatch in the timing of job destruction and job creation so that unemployment remains high for some period after the initiation of reform. These findings lead to the conclusion that globalization brings winners and losers in the labor market.

For workers to prosper in the more open economy requires different types of social protection, and this is the topic of the final section. One-time compensation programs can address the needs of those workers who lose badly. The fact that skill premiums seem to be on the rise everywhere highlights the importance of a good education system that provides opportunities for all. As for the insurance needs of workers, unemployment insurance and severance pay schemes can be effective for formal sector workers. However, the poorest people cannot be reached by such schemes because they are in the informal sector or self-employed in agriculture. They are better reached by public works programs that provide pay or food for work. The nature of social protection will have a large effect on the benefits of opening up. Countries with rigid labor markets and large public employment have benefited less from economic reform, including trade liberalization. Finally, we emphasize that countries have taken a variety of approaches to providing social protection, raising doubts as to whether there are any advantages to imposing a standard set of labor regulations through WTO sanctions, as some have proposed. We agree with developing countries that this approach is most likely to turn into a new form of protectionism that restricts opportunities for low-income countries and hence tends to keep wages in the developing world low and labor conditions there poor.

Open economies have more competition and firm turnover

AS DEVELOPING COUNTRIES HAVE LIBERALIZED FOREIGN TRADE and investment, their firms have been exposed to more competition from around the globe. For many developing countries, imports relative to national income have increased significantly. Furthermore, FDI is a large share of total investment in many economies. This is especially true for the big emerging market economies that receive the bulk of foreign investment. For the 10 emerging market economies that were the top recipients of FDI, FDI as a share of total investment increased from about 2 percent in 1970 to 17 percent in 1997 (figure 3.1). For other low- and middle-income countries FDI has also increased significantly, to about 10 percent of total investment. What is the effect of this growing competition on domestic firms? Chapter 1 presented evidence of dynamic benefits from openness that increase the growth rate of the economy. In this section we go down to a more micro level and look at the evidence concerning how openness affects firms in four significant ways.

Firm turnover. Developing countries often have large productivity dispersion across firms making similar things: high productivity and low productivity firms co-exist. A consistent finding of firm-level studies is that openness leads to lower productivity dispersion (Haddad 1993; Haddad and Harrison 1993; Harrison 1994). High-cost producers exit the market as prices fall; if these firms were less productive, or were experiencing falling productivity, then their exits represent productivity improvements for the industry. While the destruction and creation of new firms is a normal part of a well-functioning economy, attention is too often simply paid to the destruction of firms, missing half the picture. The increase in exits is only part of the adjustment—albeit the most painful part. However, unless there are significant barriers, the other side is that there are new firms entering the market. The exits are often front loaded, but the net gains over time can be substantial.

Wacziarg (1998) uses 11 episodes of trade liberalization in the 1980s to look at the issue of competition and entry. Using data on the number

Figure 3.1 FDI as share of gross domestic investment, 1970–97

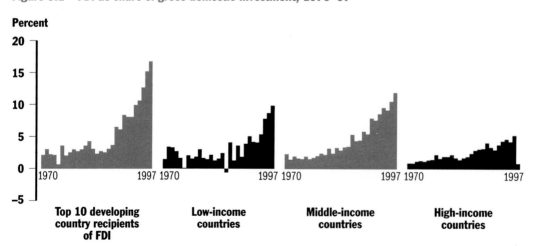

Source: World Development Indicators in Hallward-Driemeier (2001).

of establishments in each sector, he calculates that entry rates were 20 percent higher among countries that liberalized compared to ones that did not. This estimate may reflect other policies that accompanied trade liberalization such as privatization and deregulation, so this is likely to be an upper bound of the impact of trade liberalization. However, it is a sizeable effect and indicates that there is plenty of potential for new firms to respond to the new incentives.

Second, the evidence indicates that while exit rates may be significant, *net* turnover rates are usually very low. Thus, entry rates are usually of a comparable magnitude to the exit rates. Using plant level data from Morocco, Chile, and Colombia spanning several years in the 1980s, when these countries initiated trade reforms, indicates that exit rates range from 6 to 11 percent a year, and entry rates from 6 to 13 percent. Over time, the cumulative turnover is quite high, with a quarter to a third of firms having turned over in four years (Roberts and Tybout 1996). While the turnover rates are high, they are comparable to those of rich countries. Dunne, Roberts, and Samuelson (1989) report that in the United States, during any five-year period, about 35 percent of manufacturing plants will close. The phenomenon is more common among new and small firms, but even among firms with more than 250 employees, 16 percent will close (Bernard and Jensen 2001).

Third, overall exit and entry rate fluctuations are dominated by changes in the business cycle rather than by changes in trade and industrial policies. While the adjustments coming from liberalization are real, the costs should be put in context. The evidence from six semi-industrialized countries shows that the effect of fluctuations in macroeconomic conditions are more significant than the effects of trade liberalization on entry and exit rates (Roberts and Tybout 1996).

The higher turnover of firms is an important source of the dynamic benefit of openness. In general, dying firms have falling productivity and new firms tend to increase their productivity over time (Liu and Tybout 1996; Aw, Chung, and Roberts 2000; Roberts and Tybout 1996). In Taiwan, China, Aw, Chung, and Roberts find that within a five-year period, the replacement of low-productivity firms with new, higher-productivity entrants accounted for half or more of the technological advance in many Taiwanese industries.

Market structure and prices. Barriers to entry—including explicit restrictions on foreign ownership or trade barriers—can foster conditions where domestic firms retain monopoly power. The opening of the domestic market to FDI or imports can thus help to break local abuses of market power. This can have three related effects. One is that the market structure can change, with more firms producing goods if local monopolies are broken up. Second, if barriers to entry are lower, resources tend to move to the most productive areas and greater innovation is encouraged. Third, prices will likely come down as competition increases.

The effects of foreign investment on market structure are complex. Blomstrom and Kokko (1996) conclude that the balance of the evidence indicates that multinational corporations (MNCs) are more likely to crowd out local firms in developing countries, leading to higher concentration ratios on the production side. But they go on to point out that some increase in concentration ratios on the production side may not be a bad thing—particularly if it means there is better exploitation of scale economies. Provided a significant number of competitors remain, a decrease in the total number of producers may not be detrimental. If imports are produced more cost effectively than the domestic producers, some domestic products will be driven out of that range of goods. Thus, it is possible that concentration of domestic production increases, while the range of goods increases and the price of goods declines. In this case greater concentration is consistent with greater productivity and lower prices.

Increased concentration as a result of foreign investment is more of a worry if protectionist trade policies are in place. Tariffs give MNCs an incentive to "jump" the tariffs and produce locally. However, once behind the protective barriers, they can use them to shore up their own monopoly position. Thus, the best means of ensuring that such a MNC faces competition is the same as if it were a locally owned monopoly: expose it to pressures from rivals abroad. Liberalized trade can be one of the most effective means of ensuring against market power. Such a solution is most effective for traded goods. But even in areas such as non-traded services, openness to foreign bids can be a disciplining force.

The evidence is clearer for the effect of trade liberalization on market structure and prices. Many authors find that greater openness to trade leads to lower mark-ups. Some studies focus on the relationship of price mark-up and import penetration or tariff levels, looking across industries at a point in time. More convincing studies have tested the "imports as discipline" hypothesis by looking at changes in mark-ups as countries liberalize trade (Levinsohn 1993; Roberts and Tybout 1996). Both types of studies find a negative relationship between openness and mark-ups.

Data from Mexico show that with the liberalization of the late 1980s, mark-ups fell dramatically, particularly in industries with greater market concentration and a high proportion of large firms. Grether (1996) finds that a reduction in tariffs of 1 percent would lower mark-ups by up to 1.5 percent for large firms in more concentrated industries. In Chile, sectors with the greatest import penetration had the lowest price-cost mark-ups (figure 3.2).

Technology transfer and spillovers. FDI is distinct from the simple movement of capital across borders, a point industrial economists highlighted 30 years ago. Faced with options of servicing the foreign market through exports or by investing more passively with equity instruments, the question is why some firms decide to establish production facilities abroad, and why it is so important to maintain control of these affiliates. The insight is that such firms possess some intangible asset—design, technology, managerial skills, or brand image—that not only makes a foreign affiliate profitable, but that warrants maintaining control of such an entity for fear of losing the intangible asset. It is precisely the existence of this intangible asset that makes FDI attractive to host countries. It is the potential for spillovers from the assets or for the diffusion of such an asset to local producers that has made many policymakers eager to seek out foreign investors.

It is understandable why so much emphasis is placed on the potential for FDI to provide a mechanism for technology transfer when one looks

Figure 3.2   Evidence of imports-as-discipline: Chilean industries, 1980s–90s

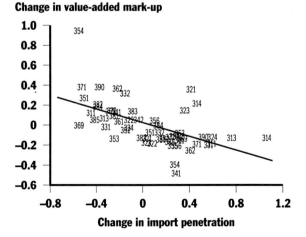

Note: Numbers of data points reflect ISIC.
Source: Hoekman, Kee, and Olarreaga (2001).

at the dominant role multinationals play in research and development and in generating new technologies. More than 80 percent of FDI originates from six countries—the United States, the United Kingdom, Japan, Germany, Switzerland, and the Netherlands. These countries are also the ones that dominate technology production. From 1970 to 1998, between 90 and 98 percent of all technology licensing and royalty payments were made to these six countries. From 1970 to 1985, more than 80 percent of payments on royalties, licenses, and patent rights to the United States were made by foreign affiliates of U.S. firms. For Germany, more than 90 percent of the payments from developing countries came from its own affiliates, while the figure for Japan was 60 percent (UNCTC 1988). These numbers underscore both the importance of MNCs as a source of research and development, and that an important part of all formal technology transfers are closely tied to FDI.

Studies in Uruguay, Mexico, and Morocco have shown that firms in sectors with a large multinational presence tend to be more productive (Kokko 1996; Haddad and Harrison 1993). However, in Venezuela, domestically owned firms did worse as MNC presence rose. This could be attributed to MNCs' initial lower local content of inputs, their siphoning off domestic demand, and their ability to hire away higher-quality labor through higher wages (Aitken and Harrison 1999). It should also be noted that as local content tends to increase over time, the potential for positive effects grows (McAcleese and McDonald 1978).

It is not likely that mere foreign presence is sufficient for spillovers. It is even possible that a large foreign presence is itself a sign of weak domestic firms, that local firms were not able to compete or absorb spillovers and so surrendered significant market share to foreign firms. What seems to be crucial is the nature of the interactions between foreign and local firms. Thus, the potential for spillovers will be greater if an affiliate of a MNC actively engages with and competes with local firms.

Kokko (1994) tests the hypothesis that spillovers should not be expected in all industries. For industries where MNCs produce in "enclaves," where neither products nor technologies bear much resemblance to local competition, there would be little spillover. However, if the competition is more direct, there are more opportunities for learning. Using Mexican data, he finds evidence of spillovers for non-enclave industries. Thus, high local competence and a competitive environment are both likely to raise the capacity of local firms to absorb technology spillovers from a greater foreign presence in the domestic market.

Studies also show a positive correlation between access to imported inputs and productivity (Handoussa 1986; Tybout and Westbrook 1995; Hallward-Driemeier, Iarossi, and Sokoloff 2000) Using data on 3,000 firms from Indonesia, Korea, the Philippines, and Thailand, Hallward-Driemeier and others find that foreign exposure significantly raises productivity. The use of foreign inputs is one such measure. It is also striking that the degree of benefits is greatest where the economy is the least developed.

Trade can be a way of importing the research and development carried out by the exporting country. Several papers examine the theoretical and empirical implications of a model where countries of the North conduct R&D and export to the South (for example, Coe, Helpman, and Hoffmiaster 1995). They estimate that spillovers of R&D from the North through trade are substantial: increasing the R&D stock in the North by $100 can raise output in the South by $25. Other papers using OECD data also find R&D spillovers through direct bilateral trade flows and through indirect channels of trade passing through third countries (Lumenga-Neso, Olarreaga, and Schiff 2001).

Attracting a multinational can also be a means of improving the quality of inputs. Their local suppliers can improve their productivity as discussed above. But, in addition, evidence shows that MNCs often encourage suppliers to relocate with them. The corollary of MNCs' local content rising over time is that their suppliers also diversify, providing high-quality inputs for the broader local market (Hallward-Driemeier 1997).

As the importance of intra-industry trade continues to grow, the ability to acquire imported inputs will be key to attracting new foreign firms interested in establishing an export platform. But allowing greater access to high-quality inputs can raise the productivity of all firms, not just the narrower set of exporting firms. For the benefits to be widely realized, it is important not to restrict the ability to import to a subset of firms such as those in export processing zones. Particularly for more backward countries, reform in this area holds some of the best promise for productivity improvements.

Learning and threshold effects of exporting. Of all the means of increasing competition with foreign firms, removing barriers to exports is most clearly beneficial for domestic firms. By selling abroad, firms can better exploit economies of scale as their market increases. They are also more exposed to new technologies and innovative means of production and face steeper competition, forcing them to be as efficient as possible. It is well accepted that firms that export are more productive on average than firms that serve only domestic markets. However, there has been a debate about whether it is the experience of exporting itself that contributes to this greater productivity or whether it is simply that more efficient firms self-select to become exporters. There have been some studies testing whether there is "learning by exporting." Bernard and Jensen (1999) find that while the level of productivity is higher for exporters, exporters' productivity growth is not significantly different from non-exporters'. While they find little evidence of "learning by exporting" for U.S. firms, they do find fixed costs of exporting so that there is a role for a firm's past export history affecting today's export decision.

Clerides, Lach, and Tybout (1998) look at Colombia, Chile, and Morocco. Other than the apparel and leather industries in Morocco, they argue that the evidence supports the self-selection hypothesis rather than that of learning by exports. However, they provide evidence that exports do provide an alternative source of spillovers. They find that if many firms in a region are exporting, all firms in the region tend to enjoy lower average costs. Bigsten and others (2000) point out that the strongest test would be to look at the evidence from small, technologically backward, and more closed economies. Firms in these environments would be those most likely to benefit from greater exporting opportunities. They would be able to realize greater scale economies and be exposed to new technologies and product types, and the effect would be greatest for firms as they first entered export markets. Using data from four African countries (on average 11 times smaller than those in the study by Clerides and others), they do find evidence of both self-selection and as well as significant learning effects. Kraay (1999) also finds significant learning effects among Chinese enterprises. However, he finds that the effect is stronger among more established exporters relative to new entrants. This is consistent with there being a number of fixed costs associated with entering export markets so that it takes time to realize the benefits of exporting.

Hallward-Driemeier, Iarossi, and Sokoloff (2000), using data from five East Asian countries, also modify the self-selection interpretation. Firms that export are indeed more productive. Rather than gaining further productivity benefits once they have already entered export markets, the benefit comes as firms try to pass the threshold and enter such markets. They find evidence that it is in aiming for export markets that firms undertake steps necessary to improve their productivity. They document the differences between firms that export and those that do not on a number of behaviors that are consistent with raising productivity, including training, using foreign technology, imported inputs, and capital intensity. As much of the productivity gains may be realized before actual entry into export markets, the measured learning effects are lower. They also find that the productivity differential between exporters and non-exporters is wider, the lower the country's per capita income, reinforcing the point that the greatest benefits of encouraging exports will be realized among the less developed countries.

The investment climate affects the benefits of openness

FIRM-LEVEL STUDIES DOCUMENT THE *POTENTIAL* FOR OPENNESS to support productivity growth at the micro level. Entrepreneurs with good ideas can exploit them over a large market. They can get access to the best machinery and inputs and be exposed to a competitive environment that encourages efficiency. We emphasize the word "potential," because reaping these benefits fully will depend very much on what we call the "investment climate." By investment climate, we mean the regulatory framework for starting up firms and expanding production, the quality of supporting infrastructure (including financial services, power, transport, and communications), and the overall economic governance (such as contract enforcement, fair taxation, and control of corruption). A location with a very poor investment climate that liberalizes foreign trade and investment is likely to get imports but not much investment and exporting. The evidence cited above shows that openness can support innovation and productivity growth, but clearly there are other important ingredients as well. There are numerous examples of the regulatory burdens facing firms in developing countries. One widely cited example was provided by the attempt of the Institute for Liberty and Democracy in Peru to register a fictitious garment plant in the 1980s. It took 289 days to register the factory and the equivalent of 23 months of minimum wages to complete the task (De Soto 1989). In this section we look at some of the factors that make up a good investment climate, how locations can improve their investment climates, and other ways in which governments try to support their firms to be more productive and competitive.

Some insight into the important elements of the investment climate comes from a recent Confederation of Indian Industries–World Bank survey covering 1,000 private firms in 10 Indian states.[1] India is a particularly interesting case study as it committed itself to substantial trade and investment liberalization in the early 1990s. Many policies are controlled at the state level, however, so there is substantial variation in the investment climate across the country. Since India is home to the largest number of people subsisting on $1 a day or less, the potential for improving the competitive environment as an effective poverty reduction tool is enormous.

Entrepreneurs in the survey were asked to identify the best and worst climate states, and to give an estimate of the cost savings of operating in different locations. The first finding of interest was that there were consistent views Maharashtra was widely recognized as providing the "best" investment climate, while West Bengal and Uttar Pradesh were seen as offering poor investment climates. Three relatively low-income states were seen as having quite good investment climates: Andhra Pradesh, Tamil Nadu, and Karnataka. The entrepreneurs perceived an overall cost saving of 30 percent between the best and worst states, a large competitive disadvantage for firms to overcome.

Quantitative information from the survey shows that the cost estimate of the entrepreneurs is quite accurate, indicating that investors are well informed about the investment climate. Controlling for sector and size, value added per worker is about 30 percent higher in the good investment climate states compared to those with a poor investment climate. Much of the difference in value added is accounted for by differences in total factor productivity. It is instructive to relate these differences in productivity to various measures of the investment climate. We will highlight three areas. The first is the relative supply and cost of infrastructure services. Electricity costs are a prime example. In Uttar Pradesh 98 percent of firms have their own generator, while less than half do in Maharashtra. Particularly for small and medium firms, this represents a large burden. Reliance on the public grid is much lower in low investment climate states owing to frequent power interruptions. As self-generation is more expensive—especially for smaller-scale enterprises—there are enormous variations in the share of electricity in total costs.

Another source of bottlenecks is the regulatory environment. There are important health and safety regulations that must be observed and a certain number of factory inspections on these grounds is desirable. However, the number of regulations and visits can become excessive. They not only represent opportunity costs for managers for the time spent with the officials, but can also be a source of corruption. The survey found that firms in poor climate states on average received twice as many visits as those in good climate states. Another important area of regulation concerns labor relations. India has had particularly stringent rules designed to protect workers, so that firms with more than 100 employees must be granted state government permission before laying off any workers. The extent to which these regulations hamper firms varies across states, with extreme lack of flexibility leading to lower productivity.

Because India has macro and trade policies set at the national level, it is a good case to highlight the effect of the investment climate at the micro level. Some states within India have better regulatory and infrastructure environments and these states are getting more foreign investment, more domestic investment (figure 3.3), and more growth. We should emphasize that an effective investment climate at the micro level is important, whether or not a country is open to foreign trade and investment. But a location that is open to the global economy, yet hampered by a poor investment climate, will not benefit much from globalization.

If effective institutions are needed to get strong benefits from openness, should countries wait until they have such institutions to open up? Not necessarily. One of the reasons why liberalization of trade in services is so important is that developing countries can use these markets to improve the investment climate. Allowing foreign firms to provide financial services, telecommunications, and power can be a good strategy for

Figure 3.3   Interstate variation in mean rate of net fixed investment

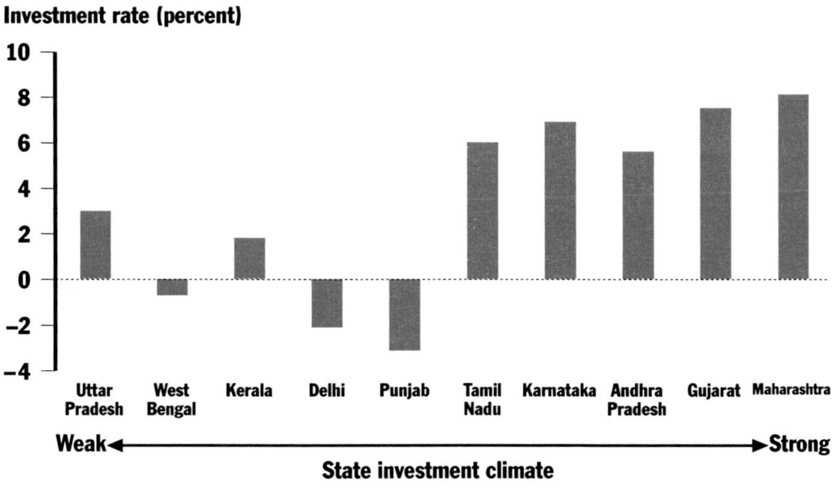

Source: Dollar and others (2001).

97

strengthening the investment climate. Also, openness to trade and investment can reduce corruption, and controlling corruption is a key part of building a good investment climate.

Services account for almost two-thirds of global GDP and only 20 percent of global trade. Many services, by their nature, are non-traded goods. They either require extensive contact with the provider, are intangible, cannot be stored, or require immediate use. Much of the foreign participation would thus be through foreign direct investment. FDI in services had lagged far behind that of manufacturing, although the increase in privatization, particularly in Eastern Europe and in Latin America, has led to substantial increases in FDI in services. The composition of the service investments is also encouraging: the vast majority are indeed in areas that are inputs to other businesses. In the late 1990s financial services, telecommunications, and infrastructure were among the top sectors attracting foreign investors, and dominated the inflows through mergers and acquisitions in developing countries.

Mishkin (2001) argues that foreign banks enhance financial development for at least three reasons. First, foreign banks have more diversified portfolios as they have access to sources of funds from all over the world, which means that they are exposed to less risk and are less affected by negative shocks to the home country economy. Second, foreign entry can lead to the adoption of best practices in the banking industry, particularly in risk management but also in management techniques, which leads to a more efficient banking sector. Third, if foreign banks are important in the banking sector, governments are less likely to bail out banks when they have solvency problems. A lower likelihood of bailouts encourages a more prudent behavior by banking institutions, an increased discipline, and a reduction in moral hazard.

Regarding foreign bank entry, Claessens, Demirgüç-Kunt, and Huizinga (1998) show that the competitive pressures created by foreign banks lead to improvements in banking system efficiency in terms of lower operating costs and smaller margins between lending and deposit interest rates. Demirgüç-Kunt, Levine, and Min (1998) contend that foreign bank entry tends to strengthen emerging markets' financial systems and lower the probability that a banking crisis will occur. The internationalization of financial services has grown rapidly in developing countries. In East Asia, Latin America, and Eastern Europe the share of total bank assets controlled by foreign banks increased several-fold during the short period from 1994 to 1999 (figure 3.4). In Eastern Europe the proportion of assets held by foreign banks passed 50 percent in 1999.

Figure 3.4 Share of total assets controlled by foreign banks in selected countries

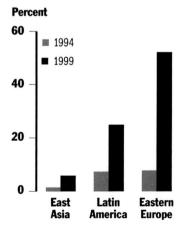

Source: Schmukler and Zoido-Lobatón (2001).

Examples show that foreign participation can contribute substantially to lower prices and improved delivery of other business services as well. Hoekman and Primo Braga (1997) document how increased competition in the provision of port services in Veracruz, Mexico, reduced costs by 30 percent and increased container turnover by 50 percent within one year. Privatization and foreign participation in Aeromexico and Mexicana raised labor productivity by 50 to 100 percent. Argentina also saw marked improvements in telecommunication services in the 1990s with FDI in the privatized market (World Bank 1997).

However, greater openness on service provision also raises special challenges. Many service areas are natural monopolies, and because they are non-traded it is less clear how to bring foreign competition to discipline behavior. One route is through negotiations on license renewals. However, if too much uncertainty revolves around the terms of agreements, investors will be unwilling to undertake the substantial fixed costs involved with establishing their operations.

If governments have decided to privatize, they still must determine whether to allow foreigners as bidders. Another decision is whether to structure the industry as a monopoly or with competition. It is thought that competition among service provides will foster greater investment than under monopoly providers, leading to faster, cheaper- and higher-quality provision. However, the potential costs include a loss of scale economies and reduced potential for cross-subsidies across locations or groups. There is also the potential that the proposal to introduce competition will lower government revenue from the sale as bidders see less opportunity for profit and so will offer a lower price to compensate for the risk. Bidders may also ask for a "temporary" exclusive license—an arrangement that may be politically difficult to change and may later be seen as no longer efficient, depending on the investment pattern of the incumbent in the intervening time.

In their analysis of privatization of telecommunications in Africa, Haggarty and Shirley (2000) show that countries are more likely to choose competition if historically service has been poor, access has been limited relative to other countries in the region, and profitability has been low. Poor service will help push governments to consider more drastic changes, and public opinion is less likely to favor the incumbent with a poor track record. If prior access has been limited, there is also more scope for a rival to enter and challenge a dominant position. Foreign bidders offer additional expertise and often higher-quality services. However, they are also more likely to ask for exclusive contracts. In assessing the trade-offs, officials must determine their ability to regulate the foreign firm to ensure that quality does improve and mark-ups are not excessive.

One area of government services that has received particularly widespread criticism is customs administration. This has long been seen as one of the agencies most likely to be corrupt. In recent years private companies have offered contracts to do pre-shipment inspections to provide an independent verification of the value of imports. While such contracts have the potential to reduce corrupt behavior, they are not foolproof. Aside from the obvious danger that private sector employees themselves could be open to bribes, exporters still know that there are odds of not being caught, or that import officials would be open to bribes when reconciling reports. Again, the quality of domestic institutions still matters in the likely success of these contracts (Johnson 2001). If indeed other agencies are less corrupt, such contracts with a private firm could provide a useful means of bringing customs administration more into line.

Given the concerns regarding market power in non-traded service sectors, government regulation and oversight will be important to ensure that quality services continue to be offered at reasonable prices. Privatization itself is not a sufficient guarantor of improvements; the nature of the regulatory framework will be important to ensure that benefits are indeed realized. But there is substantial evidence showing the potential for reliance on the international market itself to bolster weak institutions, thereby strengthening the very framework needed to maximize the benefits of wider liberalization.

Finally, many governments support individual firms or industries to try to help them compete. Protection against imports has been tried as a way to help firms become competitive: the "infant-industry argument." The fact that most developing countries have chosen to reduce import barriers suggests that they have concluded that this strategy never worked very well or at best has outlived its usefulness. To this we would add that another stylized fact about removing protection is that typically the long-protected firms have not become efficient and do not in fact survive in the more competitive environment. The experience of the Indian machine tool industry provides a case in point. It was long protected with 100 percent tariffs on imports—an "infant-industry" strategy designed to give firms time to "grow up" and become competitive. However, when import tariffs were slashed in the early 1990s as part of the overall liberalization, Indian firms were not competitive. Taiwanese producers quickly came in and took a third of the market. Since then the Indian industry has been adjusting. It has largely won back most of the lost domestic market and is now struggling to export. A recent benchmarking study of the industry shows how: productivity of Indian firms making computer-numerically controlled (CNC) lathes varies enormously (figure 3.5). The best firms have productivity close to the level of Taiwanese firms in making a standard lathe (7.5 kW)—but Indian wages for the skilled labor used in this industry are one-sixth of Taiwanese wages. So, the best Indian firms are highly cost competitive in the 7.5 kW machines and close to competitive for the larger 11 kW machines. Who are the competitive Indian firms? New entrants—not the old, protected firms. As discussed earlier, opening up this sector is likely to lead to a reduction in productivity dispersion among Indian firms, with the low-productivity firms closing or merging with more successful ones.

As protection has declined as a means of support, many governments have adopted support for exporters by means of EPZs. The number of such zones has mushroomed, from only a handful in the 1970s to more than 500 in 73 countries by 1995. Potentially, these zones can help to overcome the coordination problem—getting many firms to invest in the same place at the same time. They also provide a source of foreign exchange and employment and offer the possibility of technology

Figure 3.5   Relative productivity in machine tools

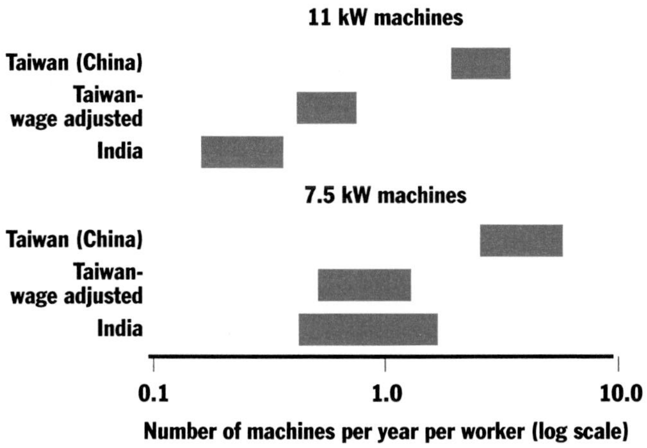

Source: Sutton (2000).

spillovers, training, and demonstration effects. Most EPZs require extensive infrastructure investments, and many firms producing there receive tax holidays as well as subsidized land or utilities. Domestic firms not located in a zone are denied the benefits those in the EPZ receive and are thus at a competitive disadvantage. There is a wide range of experience among countries, and some, such as Mauritius, have made the system work well. Sometimes they are costly and ineffective. Their potential for coordination is a useful supplement an effective investment climate, but they do not work well as a compensation for major deficiencies in the investment climate.

The technological spillovers appear to be the most difficult benefits to achieve. The extent of such spillovers depends heavily on the links that the EPZ has with local firms. Backward linkages can develop if there is sufficient reliance on local suppliers. Many firms in EPZs are motivated largely by the prospect of cheap labor, and production processes are thus labor intensive and often require low skills, reducing the potential for significant training or opportunities for learning by doing. Unless carefully designed to encourage linkages between firms inside and outside the EPZ, the potential for spillovers is limited, and reforms designed to remove barriers to exporting more generally are likely to have greater beneficial results. A further justification is sometimes put forward: that an export zone is the "best feasible option." Policymakers may recognize the benefits of dismantling various protectionist policies, but because of political pressures feel that broad liberalization is not feasible. Creating an EPZ at least allows for some firms to benefit from the relaxation of import tariffs or other restrictions. Each country is different, and in some cases EPZs may be the best option for integrating with the world market.

A related question is whether countries should be actively trying to recruit foreign firms to locate in their countries. Small, low-income countries are insufficiently noticed by large MNCs. Private foreign investment is related to perceptions of country risk, but these perceptions are often inaccurate. The published ratings such as those by *Institutional Investor*, which are based on polls of investor opinion, are systematically less favorable to Africa than is justified by the fundamentals (Ul Haque, Mark, and Mathieson 2000). Consistent with this bias in opinion, Jaspersen, Aylward, and Knox (2000) find that FDI to Africa is systematically lower than would be predicted by the fundamentals. A new element of corporate responsibility for MNCs is to look beyond

China and other emerging markets. Major companies could make a substantial difference if they located in small economies, without reducing their profitability.

In response to this problem many governments grant tax breaks or provide subsidized industrial estates to foreign firms. As with EPZs, such methods can address the coordination problem and thus be a useful supplement to an effective investment climate. Particularly if there are agglomeration effects, such that attracting an initial foreign firm brings additional foreign firms, the rationale for such a policy could be sound. However, as with EPZs, it is not clear how much countries should engage in this process. There is a real danger of suffering the "winners' curse" if the host offers too generous a package to prospective FDI firms. In their bid to attract a foreign firm the costs incurred may far outweigh any spillover benefits the multinational's domestic presence will generate. Using subsidies to compensate for a difficult investment climate can be very expensive. Argentina in the 1980s offers one extreme example. A special production zone was created in Tierra del Fuego to assemble electronic goods. Firms were given generous tax breaks and tariff subsidies. As the domestic market was highly protected, firms were able to charge prices that exceeded international ones by 150 to 400 percent. The business was so profitable that firms (both foreign and domestic) established plants in the zone, imported finished goods from Japan to Panama where they were disassembled, and imported these parts to Argentina where they were reassembled. By 1990, this program was estimated to have cost the treasury 0.5–1.0 percent of GDP (Newfarmer 2001). More generally, Lall and Streeten (1977) studied 90 foreign investments and found that more than a third reduced national income, and Encarnation and Wells (1986) had similar findings in their study of 50 projects. Until the extent of externalities is better known, our recommendation is to avoid courting foreign firms too vigorously.

Overall, there are examples of successful targeted promotions that have led to broader spillovers to the larger economy. However, too often the costs outweigh the benefits. Additionally, the danger of introducing new distortions and rent-seeking opportunities will fuel interest groups, making the political decision to reverse course that much harder. Policies that emphasize improving infrastructure and the investment climate more generally offer benefits that are open to all firms. This will promote greater efficiency and encourage more entry—of both local firms and foreign investors.

Integration with the world economy affects employment and wages

THE DISCUSSION OF FIRMS SETS THE STAGE FOR OUR NEXT issue: the welfare of workers and the need for good labor market and education policies. If much of the productivity benefit of greater global integration comes through more competitive product markets and "churning" of firms—this raises obvious concerns about workers. What is the effect of external liberalization on wages, skill premiums, unemployment, job security, and gender differentials? And what policies and programs are necessary to ensure that workers benefit from openness?

In the long run integrating with the world economy raises wages. Freeman, Oostendorp, and Rama (2001) find that the growth rate of wages has been twice as rapid in the globalizing developing countries identified in Chapter 1, as in the less globalized countries, and faster than in the rich countries as well (figure 3.6). The data used in this study, originally collected by the International Labor Office through its October Survey, have rarely been used for research purposes because of comparability problems. Freeman and Oostendorp (2000) standardized the data in a comparable format (monthly wages of men in U.S. dollars). The occupations considered by the October Survey are quite narrowly defined (for example, bricklayer), so this is a unique source for examining the effect of integration on wages properly measured. Figure 3.6 reports the average change in wages for a large number of specific occupations. This evidence shows that workers benefit strongly from the faster growth that accompanies integration.

Freeman, Oostendorp, and Rama (2001) also examine the timing of wage effects and the differential impact of trade and investment. They find that trade openness reduces wages in the short run, while direct foreign investment increases them. They estimate that the effect of greater trade on wages is negative for the first three years (figure 3.7). Thus, in an economy that liberalizes trade and gets little foreign investment (either because the investment climate is weak or simply because there is a lagged response of investors), opening up can lead to temporary declines in formal sector wages.

Several studies find that openness—especially to FDI—increases the return to education and raises the skill premium (the extra pay that skilled

Figure 3.6   Wage growth by country group

Growth between 1980s and 1990s (percent)

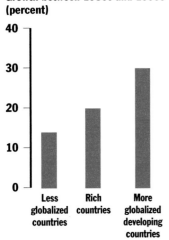

Source: Freeman, Oostendorp, and Rama (2001).

Figure 3.7   Wages and openness to trade

Changes in wages due to increased trade of 1 percent of GDP

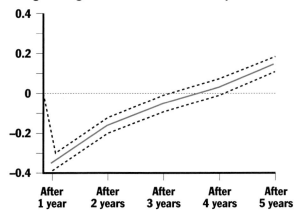

Source: Freeman, Oostendorp, and Rama (2001).

workers get relative to unskilled workers). The skill premium is usually measured as the increase in labor earnings associated with an additional year of formal education, for the average worker. This increase is also known as the return to education. Several case studies have found that the skill premium has increased in specific developing countries during periods of trade liberalization. Robbins (1997) examined wages in Colombia's seven principal cities between 1976 and 1994. He found that growth in the supply of skills lowered, and trade liberalization and real devaluation raised, wage dispersion. Robbins and Gindling (1999) present evidence that trade liberalization in Costa Rica led to an increase in the relative demand for more-skilled workers. Green, Dickerson, and Arbache (2000) examined the level and dispersion of wages, the skilled wage premium, and employment composition before and after trade liberalization in Brazil. They found a rise in the returns to college education and a decrease in the returns to intermediate levels of education. Beyer, Rojas, and Vergara (1999) showed that a positive relationship existed between returns to education and openness in Chile during 1960–96. They found that the earnings gap between college graduates and workers with primary education decreases with the share of the labor force that has college education, increases with openness, and decreases with the relative price of tradable goods (more specifically, textiles).

So, we take it as a stylized fact that the skill premium has risen in many developing countries. At first glance this may seem surprising. If unskilled labor is taken as the most abundant factor in developing countries, then one might think that trade liberalization would reduce the skill premium in these countries. There are a number of reasons why that might not be the case. First, the studies we are talking about deal with formal sector wages. If workers in protected industries are sharing in the rents from protection, then their wages are not typical of what an unskilled worker can earn. Liberalization may easily result in the loss of wages for workers in protected sectors.

Second, a common difficulty in many of these studies is to disentangle the effects of globalization from those of other shocks and policy reforms. We have emphasized that the globalizing developing countries are typically pursuing a range of reforms at once. Behrman, Birdsall, and Székely (2000) address this difficulty by considering a variety of policy reform indicators across 18 Latin American countries over the period 1980–98. These indicators are also combined in a composite reform index. Behrman, Birdsall, and Székely find that reform overall has had a short-run disequalizing effect of expanding wage differentials, although this effect tends to fade away over time. This disequalizing effect is due to the strong effect of domestic financial market reform, capital account liberalization, and tax reform. On the other hand, privatization contributed to narrowing wage differentials, and trade openness had no effect.

A third reason why the movement of the skill premium may be counter-intuitive is that, while there is evidence that countries do in fact export through trade their abundant factors, there are many factors of production and many countries, so the effect of this trade is complicated. Suppose, plausibly, that the technology embodied in direct foreign investment and skilled labor are complements. Then one important effect of trade and investment liberalization together could be to significantly raise demand for selected skilled workers—such as engineers, accountants, and finance specialists. Some evidence for this view is found in Feenstra and Hanson (1997). They analyze a panel of nine industries across Mexican states and conclude that outsourcing, under the form of *maquiladoras*, is associated with an increase in the relative earnings of non-production workers compared to production workers.

A quasi-experiment on the effect of the overall liberalization-cum-globalization package is the dramatic transition experienced by formerly planned economies in recent years. Countries in Eastern Europe and the

FSU, as well as China and Vietnam, were suddenly confronted with the unleashing of market forces, openness to trade, and FDI. The result was a dramatic increase in the returns to education (figure 3.8). The observations in this figure are drawn from a variety of studies, using data sets with different coverage and relying on a variety of econometric techniques. As a result, the estimated returns may not be strictly comparable, not even within the same country. However, there is an upward trend in all the countries considered. In some, the implicit effect of the transition on wage inequality is remarkably large. For instance, if the estimates for the Czech Republic are taken literally, the wage gap between a college-educated person and a worker with primary education increased by roughly 60 percentage points in less than one decade.

The experience of the transition economies should be seen as an upper bound, however. Their initial returns to education were abnormally low as a result of the deliberate earnings compression pursued by socialist regimes. For most developing countries confronting globalization, the initial wage inequality by skill is much higher and its probable increase much lower. More important, the increase in the returns to education is likely to be offset over time by an increase in the relative supply of educated workers. Average schooling is increasing in developing countries, and the high wage premium for college-educated workers provides an incentive to seek additional education. As a result,

Figure 3.8 Returns to education in transition economies

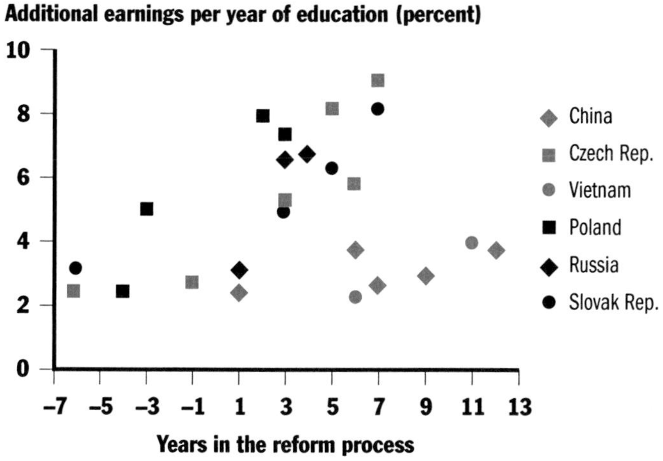

Additional earnings per year of education (percent)

Years in the reform process

China
Czech Rep.
Vietnam
Poland
Russia
Slovak Rep.

Source: Rama (2001b).

the relationship between globalization and increased returns to skill should become weaker, or even vanish, in the longer run.

The extent to which a higher skill premium does or does not persist will depend, among other things, on tax, expenditure, and education policies. Progressive taxation plus significant cost recovery in universities can reduce any incipient rise in inequality associated with opening up. Public funding of universities, especially in the absence of progressive taxation, will tend to exacerbate inequalities. It is beyond the scope of this report to go into detail about education policies, but a rise in the return to education is not necessarily a bad thing, provided that there are good educational opportunities for all levels of society. If not, globalization may lock in new inequalities. An issue we will emphasize in the next chapter is that countries and communities have plenty of freedom to design tax, expenditure, and education policies that promote equality.

Some evidence that in the long run most countries see an adjustment of the supply of skilled workers in response to the higher returns comes from the cross-sectional evidence on the returns to education and openness of the economy. Again, the estimated returns are not strictly comparable across studies, as they use different data sets, consider different control variables, and rely on different econometric techniques. But as long as the study-specific biases are independent from the openness of the economy, the pattern discerned in these studies should be basically right. Rama (2001b) finds that, cross-sectionally, returns to education do not rise with openness. If anything, they fall. Also, the dispersion of the returns seems to be smaller in more open economies, where the average wage premium is less than 10 percent per additional year of education. Much higher returns can be found in selected closed economies. Taken together, all this evidence suggests that opening up to foreign trade and investment may well lead to a higher skill premium and greater wage dispersion in the short run, but these effects are not likely to persist in the long run and, most importantly, can be addressed through other policies.

Another important point about wage inequality is that exposure to market forces can reduce the gender gap in earnings that is found in all countries. This gap can be measured as the difference in earnings between men and women that cannot be explained by differences in educational attainment or work experience. In Vietnam, at the beginning of the reform process, this gap was close to 39 percent in the private sector and 29 percent in state-owned enterprises. Five years later, in 1997–98, it had shrunk to 26 percent and 19 percent, respectively (Rama 2001a). A similar change was found in Mexico, in the context of trade liberalization. Artecona and Cunningham (2001) showed that the gender gap in earnings declined more in sectors that were more exposed to foreign competition. This evidence is admittedly scattered, but it is consistent with a non-competitive model of the labor market, where employers have some bargaining power to set wages and can therefore discriminate against women. Globalization, and the reform efforts associated with it, increase competition in product markets. This additional competitive pressure could reduce the scope for employers to set wages and discriminate against women.

Aside from effects on wages, the effects of globalization on employment are also obviously important. A series of case studies on the effects of trade liberalization shows a considerable dispersion of the net impact on employment. In Morocco, for example, employment in the average private sector manufacturing firm was basically unaffected by trade liberalization (Currie and Harrison 1997). The shift in labor demand was modest in Mexico as well (Revenga 1997). But in Uruguay, in a period when trade union activities were banned, the decline was substantial. During that period, reducing the protection rate within a sector by 1 percent led to an employment reduction of between 0.4 and 0.5 percent within the same year. The employment effect became much smaller when trade union activities were allowed (Rama 1994).

Small declines in employment may hide substantial job churning, however. The contrast between studies at the industry level and at the firm level is revealing in this respect. Seddon and Wacziarg (2001) used industry-level data to examine the impact of trade liberalization episodes on movements of labor across sectors. Their study found some labor reallocation between narrowly defined manufacturing activities. But the estimated effects were statistically insignificant and small in magnitude. On the other hand, Levinsohn (1996) used firm-level data to examine the pattern of job creation and job destruction in Chile during trade liberalization. While net employment in manufacturing fell by about 8 percent, in all years in this period about a quarter of all workers changed jobs. However, the effects of trade liberalization itself appear to be modest compared to those due to macroeconomic shocks.

Globalization also affected the nature of jobs in formerly protected sectors. In Morocco there were significant employment losses in specific groups of firms, which started to rely more on low-pay, temporary workers. The share of temporary employment in manufacturing rose by nearly 20 percentage points between 1984 and 1990. In Mexico trade reform reduced the rents available to be captured by firms and workers. As a result, an average tariff reduction of 20 percentage points led to an implied wage reduction of more than 5 percent. In Uruguay trade liberalization was associated with lower wages in the period when trade unions were not active, despite the considerable reduction in employment. In the period with active unions, the membership rate was strongly correlated with tariff barriers and concentration at the industry level. This correlation suggests that workers in protected sectors enjoy higher wages than their counterparts in sectors exposed to foreign competition.

Overall, these studies show that there was pervasive rent sharing between the protected enterprises and their workers. The removal of trade barriers makes workers lose those rents, either because they lose their jobs altogether, or because the rent attached to their jobs becomes smaller. This interpretation is consistent with the one offered for the effect of globalization on the gender gap in earnings. In both cases increased competition in product markets appears to reduce the size of labor market rents enjoyed by either employers or employees.

While globalization results in some workers losing their jobs, it leads to substantial job creation as well. The most visible part of this creation is associated with FDI—in some cases in export processing zones. EPZs have been a powerful engine for generating employment in a number of countries. The case of Mauritius is outstanding: EPZs account for 17 percent of employment. But the share is considerable in several other countries as well, especially when taking into account that agricultural activities and the informal sector still employ a considerable share of the labor force. EPZ employment shares in the mid-1990s were 5 percent in the Dominican Republic and 2–4 percent in Mexico, Honduras, and Costa Rica.

Most of the jobs in EPZs are held by women. In the Caribbean zones approximately 80 percent of the workforce is female, and the percentage is almost as high in the Philippines. This female bias is especially strong in garment production. The pattern is similar in countries that have not relied massively on EPZs, but where exporting firms have tapped local labor markets, attracting workers from surrounding villages. Industries such as textiles and electronics have massively hired young, literate, largely single women, who frequently ended up earning more than in traditional sectors like agriculture and cottage industries (World Bank 2001b). This female bias has been observed even out of the wage sector. Evidence from Ghana and Uganda reveals that women had substantial economic mobility in response to economic reforms. In these two countries rural women became increasingly engaged in non-farm employment activities, moving into the non-farm sector at faster rates than men (World Bank 2001b).

To the extent that globalization does translate into significant job creation in developing countries, the potential impact on poverty can be dramatic. But this impact depends significantly on where job creation occurs. In China much of the impetus for the rapid economic growth during the 1980s came from a tremendous expansion of rural township and village enterprise activities. These firms often emerged out of the community-level structures that had been in place before the introduction of the household responsibility system in agriculture in the late 1970s and typically became involved in labor-intensive, export-oriented manufacturing activities (Byrd and Lin 1990). The inroads into rural poverty that were achieved in China during this period were nothing short of remarkable (World Bank 2000c). In other parts of the developing world a similarly strong negative relationship between poverty and growth of the rural, non-farm sector has been observed. Even where non-farm employment opportunities accrue primarily to the relatively educated and skilled (and thus non-poor), benefits to the poor are often still discernable. This is due to the relationship between the wage rates earned by agricultural laborers in rural areas, who are generally highly represented among the poor, and the tightening of rural labor markets, which generally accompanies an expanding non-farm sector (Lanjouw and Lanjouw forthcoming).

While globalization prompts both job destruction and job creation, the timing of these two processes might not be synchronized. In such diverse countries as Chile, Mauritius, Poland, and Sri Lanka unemployment remained stubbornly high for several years after the launching of economic reforms. In the long run open economies do not appear to have higher unemployment rates. In Latin America, during two decades of increased exposure to foreign trade and international capital movements, there was only a mild upward trend in unemployment rates. The increase was dramatic in a few countries, such as Argentina, Colombia, and Paraguay. But the median rate grew by only one percentage point (World Bank 2000a). This relative stability stands in contrast to the popular perception, as reflected in opinion polls. Risk of unemployment ranks as one of the main concerns voiced by those surveyed, in most of the region.

The overall picture is that globalization leads to higher wages in developing countries, indicating that workers share in the benefits of higher productivity, but some people do lose out, especially in the short run. We emphasized in Chapter 1 that opening up does not systematically lead to higher household income inequality, indicating that the losers do not come disproportionately from the poor. Some of the losers will be formal sector workers who are relatively high up in the income distribution. Conversely, some of the winners will be poor people who get new jobs created by globalization. But some of the winners will also be highly educated engineers and accountants, and some of the losers are bound to come from the ranks of the poor. The diffuse nature of the potential losers highlights the need for extensive systems of social protection.

Social protection in globalizing economies

AS GLOBALIZATION CAN CREATE LOSERS AS WELL AS WINNERS, it is important to identify what can be done to reduce and mitigate the adverse impact of reforms aimed at integrating the economy more closely with the rest of the world. A large array of government interventions has been tried in the developing world, and the lessons learned in one country could prove useful in others. Some of these interventions are intended to help workers cope with losing their jobs. Others could be used to limit the negative effects of globalization on specific groups of workers and households.

First, a major reform program may have some identifiable big losers—workers earning large rents from protection. Even though these groups are not typically poor, it can be socially efficient to provide significant one-time compensation in order to make reforms move more smoothly. Otherwise, big losers will be vocal and concentrated opponents of reform.

Second, permanent programs to help workers cope with job loss may be established—the most obvious example being unemployment insurance. A growing number of voices advocate setting up of this kind of program in middle-income developing countries. This contrasts with the widespread criticisms of unemployment insurance in some industrial societies, where several studies have shown that long-lasting unemployment benefits encourage the unemployed to stay out of a job. Analysts who extrapolate from this developed country evidence to the situation of the new globalizers suggest that governments should introduce a mandatory savings account program instead of bringing in unemployment insurance. Such savings plans can be part of the old-age pension system, with pension benefits dependent on past contributions. Workers are able to add any unused savings to their old-age pension account and to run down their old-age pension entitlement in the event of job loss. However, extrapolation from rich country experience may not be justified. Both the adverse incentive effects of unemployment insurance and the merits of individual savings accounts might be much less than anticipated in low-income societies. When the informal sector is large, as in nearly all poor countries, it is very difficult to monitor that the beneficiaries are really unemployed. Therefore, unemployment benefits at worst create an incentive to stay out of the formal sector, not to stay out of a job. As regards mandatory savings accounts, they do not involve any risk pooling, only a spreading of the earnings loss from unemployment over the life cycle. If workers become unemployed while they are still young and exhaust their pension account, they might not have enough resources to cope with losing a job. If they are allowed to run their pension account into debt, they face an incentive to become unemployed, take on as much debt as possible, and withdraw from the formal sector to avoid repaying their debt.

Neither unemployment insurance nor mandatory savings accounts programs reach the poorest workers. Table 3.1 summarizes the findings of a comparative study on income support programs for the unemployed in Latin America (World Bank 2000a). This region has experience with a variety of programs, and can be seen as a laboratory by other middle-income countries. Table 3.1 shows that, among the workers covered by unemployment insurance in Brazil and by mandatory savings accounts

Table 3.1   Income support programs for the unemployed

Program and country	Workers legally covered by the program	Spending per beneficiary (US$)	Cost of the program falls on	Share of beneficiaries by earnings or consumption quintile (%)				
				Poorest	2nd poorest	Middle	2nd richest	Richest
Public works in Argentina	In principle, all	3,100	Taxpayers	78.6	15.3	3.5	2.1	0.4
Training in Mexico	Eligible on age, education	393	Taxpayers	69.9	15.5	8.1	5.0	1.5
Severance pay in Peru	Salaried, with given seniority	760	Workers and employers	4.7	9.5	28.6	33.3	23.8
Unemployment insurance in Brazil	Salaried in social security	664	Workers and employers	10.6	24.6	19.1	25.1	13.6
Individual accounts in Colombia	Salaried in social security	—	Workers	0.0	4.3	n.a.	19.1	76.6

— Not available.
n.a. Not applicable.
Source: World Bank (2000a).

in Colombia, very few belong to the population group with the lowest earnings or consumption. However, both these income support programs are well suited for workers in protected industries, who are usually enrolled in a social security program.

A third type of social protection is income support programs tailored to reach the poorest workers. Public works, like the Maharashtra employment guarantee scheme in India and the *Trabajar* program in Argentina, are among them (Ravallion, Datt, and Chaudhuri 1993; Datt and Ravallion 1994; Jalan and Ravallion 1999). Some training programs for the unemployed, like *Probecat* in Mexico, also fall in this category (Wodon and Minowa 2001). One common feature of these programs is that participants do not need to be enrolled in any social security program. Another important feature is the self-selection of their participants. Well-designed public works programs pay less than the average labor earnings of those unskilled workers who do have a job. As a result, only those really in need are willing to take them.

The main difference between these programs is the nature of the activities the beneficiaries must undertake. In one case they are requested to do physically demanding, full-time work. In the other they have to take full-time training. The actual productivity of these activities is subject to debate, and the non-labor component of their cost can differ substantially. But both kinds of programs seem well geared to help informal sector workers cope with job loss. As table 3.1 shows, most of their beneficiaries belong to the poorest population groups.

In between these two extremes mandatory severance pay is the most common income support program available to the unemployed in developing countries. In this program an employer is liable to pay a certain amount of money to a worker dismissed due to no fault of his or her own. The amount is usually related to the last salary of the worker and his or her seniority in the job by a formula typically involving a minimum seniority and a maximum payment. This program does not require the involvement of a social security agency. Compliance is complaint driven, which often overburdens labor inspectors but is probably cheaper than running a full-blown unemployment insurance program. Mandatory severance pay makes the employer assume the role of an insurer. If that the firm goes bankrupt, workers usually have priority over other creditors.

One potential problem with mandatory severance pay is that it may discourage hiring. This program raises separation costs in bad times, which can make employers reluctant to recruit in good times. In its extreme form, mandatory severance pay becomes equivalent to lifetime job security. In the cases of India and Zimbabwe it has been shown that lifetime job security reduces labor demand in the formal sector (Fallon and Lucas 1991). In a similar vein a cross-country study by Heckman and Pagés (2000) shows a link between high separation costs and low employment-to-population ratios, at least for young workers. However, a study focusing on the change in earnings experienced by Peruvian workers as they move from jobs covered by severance pay to non-covered jobs, or vice-versa, suggests that workers may "pay" for coverage through lower wages (MacIsaac and Rama 2001). If part of the burden falls on workers, the adverse employment effect could be alleviated or even off-set. Table 3.1 shows that mandatory severance pay, much the same as unemployment insurance, benefits mainly higher-income workers.

Finally, active labor market programs are often set up to help unemployed workers find new jobs. Training, counseling, placement services, and assistance in job search are among the most common examples. While active labor market programs of this sort are quite popular with governments, trade unions, and the general public, their effectiveness seems limited. For instance, Mexico's *Probecat* appears to be effective at providing income support to the unemployed, but not at improving their earnings ability (Wodon and Minowa 2001). The effectiveness of these programs is difficult to assess, as participants are self-selected. Workers who are more eager to succeed, or more able to learn, are more likely to participate. It is therefore difficult to disentangle the effects of the program from those of the ability of its participants. In any event the effects uncovered appear to be generally modest, and concentrated in relatively narrow subsets of participants (Fretwell, Benus, and O'Leary 1999; Gill, Fluitman, and Dar 2000).

For some workers, the negative effect of globalization takes the form of a drop in earnings, rather than a job loss. The minimum wage is a potential way to circumscribe this drop. However, the actual impact of this intervention is often exaggerated. To begin with, minimum wages are not directly relevant for the self-employed and those working in house-hold industries. In many developing countries this group represents a majority of the labor force, and it includes most of the poor. As regards salaried workers, many among those who may suffer from trade liberal-ization and deregulation earn substantially more than the minimum wage. The latter might thus be ineffective in their case.

Another important shortcoming of minimum wages as effective means of social protection in developing countries is the limited ability of governments to enforce them. Several case studies show that compliance is partial at best, even in countries with a relatively high administrative capacity (Gindling and Terrell 1995; Maloney and Fajnzylber 2000). As a result, attempts to raise labor earnings through minimum wage hikes, as in Indonesia during the early 1990s, have been quite ineffective (Rama 2001c). The flip side of weak enforcement is that the disemployment effects of minimum wages have been modest, too. In Mexico the minimum wage is so low compared to the average wage of formal sector workers that its variation has no noticeable impact on employment. Even in Colombia, where minimum wages are much higher, the estimated disemployment effects are only about one-tenth of those found in industrial countries (Bell 1997).

Rodrik (1998) finds that bigger governments, and especially bigger public sector employment, can be used as a substitute for insurance or other forms of social protection. He shows that a positive correlation exists between an economy's exposure to international trade and the size of its government. This correlation holds for most measures of government spending, in low- as well as high-income samples, and is robust to the inclusion of a wide range of controls. His explanation is that government spending plays a risk-reducing role in economies exposed to a significant amount of external risk. One piece of evidence in favor of this interpretation is that the relationship between openness and government size is strongest when terms-of-trade risk is highest.

A similar correlation exists between government employment and openness (Rodrik 1998). "Secure" jobs in the public sector could thus be seen as a form of insurance against the external risk faced by the economy, especially when those who hold those jobs transfer resources to their extended families. But this interpretation is to some extent problematic. While some public sector jobs might have been created with the deliberate goal of providing income security, other explanations are equally plausible. Preliminary work with an expanded version of the database used by Rodrik suggests that the political regime, income inequality, and the degree of ethno-linguistic fractionalization are good predictors of the share of the labor force employed by the public sector (Chong and Rama 2001). An inflated public sector can have large detrimental effects on economic performance, as discussed below.

How a government goes about providing social protection will have a large effect on how its economy performs and how much its people benefit from global integration. A cross-country study of economic growth during periods of economic reform found that some of the government interventions discussed in the previous section can lead to poor performance, while others are relatively benign (Forteza and Rama 2001). Countries with large public sector employment got poor results from reform, while the level of minimum wages or the generosity of social security benefits did not appear to have any adverse effect. These results are consistent with a "political" interpretation of the role of public sector employment in the reform process. In developing countries a large portion of the formal sector is often made up of public sector employees. Workers in protected industries also tend to be unionized. These two groups stand to lose from reforms such as trade liberalization, market deregulation, or privatization of state-owned enterprises. The more powerful they are, the more likely that reforms will be first delayed, and once they are adopted, implemented only half-heartedly. This political interpretation suggests that the payoffs to the compensation of those who stand to lose from globalization can be large. It also implies that using public sector employment as an insurance mechanism against increased economic volatility carries the risk of entrenching the forces that oppose reform. On the other hand, minimum wages and generous social security benefits do not appear to be costly.

The last labor issue that we take up concerns core labor standards. All 175 members of the International Labour Organisation have endorsed core labor standards, as a result of their acceptance of the "Declaration on Fundamental Principles and Rights at Work." These standards include a ban on abusive child labor. Obviously, this ban is not successfully enforced in very poor countries. Why? There is pervasive evidence that poverty is the primary cause of child labor. Household surveys show that, within developing countries, child labor declines sharply with family income. In Vietnam, for example, the extent of work by children aged 6 to 15 had a clear relationship to household income in a 1993 survey (figure 3.9). (Most of this work is on the family farm.) The figure also shows the 1998 extent of child labor for the same households. During the period that Vietnam was opening up to the global economy there was a sharp drop in child labor. Why? The change can be explained almost completely by the increase in household income. Over this relatively short period of time the income of the poorest 10 percent of the population increased more than 50 percent in real terms, which led to a sharp decline in child labor (and a corresponding increase in school enrollment rates).

Figure 3.9   Child labor and household consumption levels in Vietnam

Share of 6–15-year-olds working (percent)

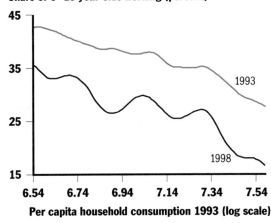

Source: Edmonds (2001).

This finding sheds important light on the current debate about core labor standards. Developing countries fear that trying to enforce labor or other standards through WTO sanctions will become a new form of protectionism that will limit their trade. With fewer trading opportunities the income of poor families will fall, increasing child labor. Thus, an apparently well-intentioned policy, such as trade sanctions against poor countries that have child labor, could easily backfire and result in more child labor.

Another important point is that developing countries are addressing problems of child labor in their own ways, with positive programs. For example, Bangladesh's Food-for-Education (FFE) program, which provides poor families with food as long as they send their young children to school, has resulted in a drop in child labor (figure 3.10). There is also evidence that the quality of schooling is important, so that improved schools lead to less child labor. Thus, there are positive programs to address this important problem, and we do not just have to wait for incomes to rise to abolish abusive child labor. These programs, however, do require resources.

This evidence raises serious concerns about the proposal to regulate child labor or other labor issues through WTO sanctions—in other words, to allow rich countries to bring unfair trade practice suits against poor countries if there is evidence of child labor. It is very unlikely that such

Figure 3.10   Bangladesh's Food-for-Education (FFE) program and child labor

Percent of school-aged children

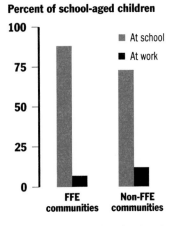

Source: Ravallion and Wodon (2000).

sanctions would reduce child labor as long as the underlying problem of poverty is not addressed. However, were the ban to be enforced on poor families, they would be worse off if no other assistance were provided. Developing countries have a good argument that there is a danger that labor standards could become a new form of protectionism against poor countries—with the ironic effect of increasing poverty and hence child labor. We emphasized in Chapter 2 that poor countries have difficulty defending their interests in the WTO, so that there is potential for these standards to be used against them to restrict their trade. If first world citizens care about child labor, it would be more constructive if they contributed money to support programs to improve schools and help poor families send their children to those schools.

More generally, there are two complementary strategies to raising labor standards. The first is to support the fundamental processes of growth that will raise labor productivity. This raises wages, not just in the firms that happen to export, but across the economy. The second is to support specific measures of social protection that benefit workers both directly and by strengthening their bargaining power. For example, health and safety standards should be set at a level where they can be enforced across the economy, not just in export enclaves. The imposition of sanctions and penalties by rich countries on the exports of poor countries would be a form of taxation, threatening these strategies rather than supporting them.

Summary of recommendations

TO STRENGTHEN THE POTENTIAL BENEFITS OF OPENNESS, developing countries need a good investment climate in which firms can start up and prosper. A good investment climate is particularly important for small and medium enterprises that will create the bulk of new jobs. Elements of a sound investment climate include efficient but streamlined regulations for entry and exit, a healthy financial system, good infrastructure, and good economic governance (contract enforcement, tax administration, safeguards against corruption). Many successfully globalizing developing countries are using the international market for services to strengthen the investment climate. Foreign trade and/or investment can help develop financial services, accounting, telecommunications, power, ports, customs administration, and other critical areas of infrastructure.

Integration with the global economy increases the return to education. This can be a good thing, provided that that there is a sound education system providing services to all. The rapid growth in new globalizing economies generates resources that can be used to strengthen the delivery of education and health services, so that the poor can participate in this growth and benefit from it. A good education system that provides opportunities for all is critical for success in this globalizing world.

The more dynamic environment calls for new types of social protection. To get reforms underway may require one-time compensation schemes for workers who would otherwise lose in a big way. Well-designed unemployment insurance and severance pay systems can provide protection to formal sector workers in an environment that will now have more entry and exit of firms. But the poorest people are better reached through self-targeting programs such as food-for-work schemes. Social protection is important not just to help individual families that lose in the more dynamic economy, but also to create a solid social foundation from which people—especially poor people—feel comfortable taking risks and pursuing entrepreneurship.

Note

1. This study provides a wealth of information of firm characteristics and the impact of government policies and the business environment on firm performance. It is a blueprint for studies that the World Bank will be supporting in additional countries in the coming years. Such databanks will provide for international comparisons, allowing for quantitative measures to complement existing qualitative rankings. For more information and access to the data, please visit the webpage: http://www.worldbank.org/research/facs/.

CHAPTER FOUR

Power, Culture, and the Environment

LOBALIZATION IS NOT JUST AN ECONOMIC phenomenon. It changes power relationships, cultures, and the environment. This chapter considers these effects.

Globalization and power

GLOBALIZATION CHANGES POWER RELATIONSHIPS. AT THE level of international relations, it changes the power of developing countries relative to that of developed countries. At the level of domestic politics, it changes the power relations between government, business, and civil society. Most fundamentally, it changes the prospects for peace—both within countries and between them.

Globalization and the international distribution of power

Undoubtedly, the first two waves of globalization—the period up to 1980—increased the power of the rich countries relative to others. This was a concomitant of widening inequality between countries. As discussed in Chapter 2, international institutions such as the GATT were created by and for rich countries. Even during this period, the club of rich countries was open to new non-western members: Japan became a major global force. However, the global institutional architecture inherited from this period is unsatisfactory and gives too little power to developing countries.

During the third wave of globalization, economic power is shifting away from the industrial countries for the first time in more than a century. The economies of the new globalizers are growing far more rapidly than those of the OECD economies: China and India are set to become major economic powers. Developing countries have a strong interest in the evolution of the global architecture because it curtails the imbalance of power. For example, the WTO offers weak countries their best prospect of forcing powerful countries to adhere to international rules rather than just doing whatever happens to suit them. It is the weak, not the strong, who are advantaged by rule-based systems of conduct.

Globalization and the domestic power of government

In some respects globalization restricts the choices open to a government. However, it is sometimes suggested that in order to succeed the new globalizers have only one choice—to model themselves on the pattern of limited government that characterizes the United States. The most obvious reason why successful globalization presents choices much greater than this is that many countries have already succeeded with a diversity of strategies. Consider two important dimensions of development: government expenditure as a share of GDP and the distribution of income. A number of highly open industrial economies have per capita incomes approximately equal to that of the United States. Among those countries with approximately the same living standards as the United States, five stand out as having radically more equal distributions of income: Austria, Belgium, Denmark, Japan, and Norway. All have Gini coefficients of around or below 0.25, contrasting with 0.41 in the United States. Like the United States, all these societies have provided an effective climate for private economic activity for a long time, but they differ in the role they assign to government. The share of GDP accounted for by central government expenditure ranges from 20 percent in the United States to 46 percent in Belgium, although the low U.S. share misses its large state-level expenditures that would bring its true figure to around 30 percent. The average share of government expenditure in GDP for low- and middle-income developing countries is only 20 percent. Hence, any of these six models of high-income success would involve governments expanding their size not only in absolute terms as GDP grows, but relative to GDP. The five high-income, high-equity societies do not constitute a common model. Nor can their markedly greater equity necessarily be attributed to their higher share of public spending. However, they do illustrate that successful globalization does not require adoption of any single, standard institutional model.

Even within the EU, a group of countries far more integrated than will be achieved globally in the foreseeable future, wide variations in taxation and social policies co-exist without serious consequences. The main social effect of the EU has been the swift reduction in poverty in the poorest of its member countries.

Globalization is consistent with a wide range of choice in social policies, but it undoubtedly reduces choice in macroeconomic management. Because of capital market integration, most governments are less free to try to smooth the business cycle through fiscal and monetary expansion during downturns. An exception is the United States, because of its key currency role (its recent tax and interest rate cuts would have triggered a threat to the currency in most countries). However, this is a less drastic loss of power than it might seem. Many governments are now skeptical of their ability to fine-tune the business cycle irrespective of the problems introduced by capital market integration.

In some respects globalization empowers capital at the expense of government and workers. Capital can now move between countries, and a single location for production can serve many national markets. As a result, governments can find themselves competing against each other to attract the single plant that will serve the market for an entire region. Such competition is limited: tax policy is not usually a major influence on location. Governments that provide a good all-around climate for investment will not have to offer special tax concessions for most investments. The way to redress the balance of power is for governments within a region to agree on some floor to their own behavior. For example, Caribbean governments found themselves in competition with each other over attracting cruise ships to visit. The shipping companies did not want to pay charges for the environmental pollution that they caused and tried to play off each island against the others. In response the Caribbean governments were able to agree on and enforce a set of port charges for cruise ships. In such ways inter-government action can offset the power of capital.

In other respects, however, globalization weakens the power of capital. One way is through the intensification of competition. In a small national market there will often be a single dominant firm, and in such markets it is relatively easy to form cartels. As firms from other countries become credible competitors, the power of locally dominant firms is reduced. We have noted the striking evidence for this in that the mark-ups that firms charge over cost have fallen. Even here globalization is not an unmitigated good: sometimes even at the global level an industry is dominated by a monopoly or a cartel. Currently, the regulation of monopolies and cartels is done at national level and so global market power is in a sense above scrutiny. The recent proposed takeover by the world's largest company, General Electric, of another large company, Honeywell, illustrates the current weakness of global governance, pitting a European regulatory authority against U.S. companies, and thus turning an issue of global regulation into a matter of rival national interests. However, the introduction of global regulation of monopolies and cartels would be politically difficult and not unambiguously beneficial for all developing countries.

A further way in which the power of capital has been reduced is through the globalization of information—"globalization from below." Companies are now far more vulnerable to international public opinion because people have learned how to harness their potential power as consumers. For example, the large company De Beers changed its policies in one market as a result of pressure from consumers in a different market. De Beers feared that there would be a diamond boycott in the United States, modeled on the fur boycott, and in response completely changed its policy toward purchasing diamonds in Africa. Nor is this power confined to the public of the industrial world. In Indonesia consumer pressure has proven effective in forcing companies to abide by local environmental standards. Again, this is not an unmitigated good. Consumers often make decisions based on very little information. Non-accountable non-governmental organizations (NGOs) can sometimes exploit this ignorance to pursue their own agendas at the expense of poor people. They threaten boycotts to enforce rich country standards that would prevent poor countries from breaking into global markets for manufactures, or shut peasants out of rich country markets for food. There is no prospect of such behavior being regulated: the only defense against abuse is to raise the level of understanding of how poor people can benefit from participating in the global economy.

Globalization and state failure

Interdependence through trade reduces international war. This is an old idea but it has been supported by quantitative research. Polachek

(1992, 1997) found that a doubling of trade between two countries reduces the risk of war and terrorism (see box 4.1) between them by 17 percent. However, the overwhelming majority of large-scale violent conflict is now due to civil war rather than international war, and the effects of globalization cannot be presumed to be benign.

During the third wave of globalization, developing countries have divided into two divergent groups in terms of economic performance. This

---

Box 4.1 Globalization and terrorism

THE INTERNATIONALIZATION OF TERRORISM IS AN instance of how global risks have outpaced global policy.

In the early 1970s there was a wave of terrorism that spread through imitation. As governments responded by protecting obvious targets, terrorists substituted bombing for hijacking, and civilian for military targets (Enders and Sanders, 2000). However, the main terrorist groups were national, such as Baader-Meinhof in Germany, Red Brigades in Italy, and Action Directe in France. Gradually, appropriate national counter-terrorist measures completely defeated them. Terrorism has used globalization to create two loopholes in these controls.

First, by spreading their organization across national boundaries, terrorists have made national-level, counter-terrorist activity less effective. Countering terrorism has become a global public good with all the attendant problems. Like other global public goods, it has been woefully under-provided. Governments have tolerated terrorists on their soil as long as their own citizens were not being targeted, and have failed to share information and coordinate efforts.

The second way in which terrorism has globalized to evade controls is to seek safe haven in the failed states that have mushroomed in recent decades—territory outside the control of any recognized government. The threat of military action is less effective against these governments: the state has already been destroyed.

The same counter-terrorist measures that defeated national terrorism will be needed to defeat international terrorism. But they will not work well unless they are conducted at a global rather than a national level. Before September 11th only four states had ratified the United Nations' convention against terrorism. To restore failed states to government, and to prevent other states from failing, will require developmental interventions. Economic decline is a major precursor to state failure, and conversely, economic progress helps to secure the state.

Because failed states can be safe havens for terrorists, economic development will be a core part of the long-term strategy to counter international terrorism. However, there is no facile connection between poverty and terrorism. Commonly, as with Baader-Meinhoff, terrorists are from wealthy and educated elites. Poor people are not the perpetrators of terrorism, but its victims. The attacks of September 11th have damaged the economic prospects for developing countries. On current forecasts in 2002 there will be around 10 million more people in poverty as a result of the attacks. Were the terrorism campaign to be sustained, its impact on poverty would be far greater—for example, an estimate of the cost of prolonged terrorism in the Basque region suggests that it has reduced income by 10 percent (Abadie and Gardeazabal, 2001). The 10 million additional people in poverty are among the unacknowledged and unidentified victims of international terrorism. Rich countries can offset these consequences through the policies of trade and aid discussed in Chapter 2.

same division applies to the more fundamental issue of violent civil conflict. It is exemplified by the differing experiences of Africa and the other developing regions. In 1970 Africa had a lower incidence of large-scale violent conflict than other developing regions. By the late 1990s Africa's incidence of conflict had risen, while that of the rest of the developing world had fallen sharply. Africa now has a much higher incidence of conflict than other developing regions.

These two diverging experiences are related: diverging economic structures are influencing the ability of the state to secure peace. New research shows that there are powerful risk factors that make marginalized countries more vulnerable to violent conflict. Collier and Hoeffler (2001) analyze all civil wars since 1960 to identify the characteristics that typically make conflict more likely.

First, the economic decline experienced by the marginalized countries is itself a major risk factor. They find that both the level of income and its rate of growth have important effects on the risk of conflict. Both low income and falling income increase the risks substantially. Since sustained economic decline results in low income, the poor growth experience of the less globalized developing countries over the past two decades has increased risk twice over. Conversely, among the globalizers the acceleration of growth and its resulting higher levels of income have considerably reduced the risk of conflict.

Second, the failure of the marginalized countries to diversify their exports into manufactured goods and services has increased their risk of conflict. Collier and Hoeffler find that, controlling for other factors, higher dependence on primary commodity exports increases the risk of conflict very substantially. There are various reasons why primary commodity exports might have this effect. By occupying the area in which primary commodities are produced, a rebel group can finance its activities through extortion. Sometimes the looting of primary commodities might even be a motivation for the rebellion. Additionally, governments get large revenues from taxing primary commodity exports and these revenues are often associated with poor governance, which in turn might induce rebellion. During third wave globalization, developing countries as a whole were able to diversify their exports massively: primary commodities as a share of their exports fell from about 75 percent in 1980 to around 20 percent by 1998. This substantially reduced the risk of conflict. But the marginalized countries did not share in this trend. Africa actually increased its dependence on primary commodities. Collier and Hoeffler find that Africa's rising risk of conflict is fully accounted for by its deteriorating economic performance.

Not only are conflicts more likely to start, they are less likely to end: conflicts are tending to get longer (Collier, Hoeffler, and Soderböm 2001). A possible explanation for this is the growth of the global trade in small arms. Thirty years ago rebel groups needed to forge a political alliance with a foreign government in order to get access to arms; now they can arm themselves directly on the private market. Basic military equipment became radically cheaper as a result of the collapse of the Warsaw Pact. A recent report estimates that more than $30 billion worth of equipment has been unofficially sold from Ukraine alone.

Not only are conflicts less likely to end, but once ended, they are likely to restart: the typical post-conflict country has a 50 percent risk of going back into conflict within five years. As a result, once a country falls into conflict it tends to become trapped into long and repeated conflict. In turn, conflict makes it far more difficult to integrate into the global industrial economy. Too many countries have become trapped in a cycle of conflict, poverty, and dependence on primary commodities.

What can be done to break this cycle? At the global level two strategies are feasible and could be effective: better governance for key markets and enhanced aid for countries at risk of conflict.

The market on which most attention has been focused is that for diamonds. Some rebel groups have clearly financed their activities from the sale of alluvial diamonds. Since there are only a few centers for cutting diamonds and relatively limited channels of distribution, it is possible to regulate the diamond market in order to make it possible to sell conflict diamonds only at a deep discount. Both De Beers and the United Nations have been active in devising methods of market regulation. As with all such regulation, initial steps are easily evaded, but with persistence it should be possible gradually to separate conflict diamonds from the legitimate market. At the other extreme of regulation, the market for cocaine is also financing rebel groups. In Colombia rebel revenues are estimated at $500 million per year. The attempt to curtail consumption in rich countries by imposing penalties on production in poor countries has created a demand for territory outside the control of governments (Brito and Intriligator 1992). Rebel organizations gain control of territory and extract a rent for permission to produce cocaine.

A further commodity where there is active international involvement is oil. In a few countries oil revenues do not even reach the government budget, but are siphoned off by corruption. Oil companies are beginning to adopt better practices of transparency so that civil society within countries can scrutinize what happens to oil income. NGOs such as Global Witness have shown that it is possible through a combination of corporate disclosure and public pressure to effect a major improvement in the governance of natural resources. Such alliances between NGOs, international corporations and the international financial institutions are part of the emerging informal global economic architecture.

In tandem with better global regulation OECD governments can reduce the risk of violent conflict in the high-risk developing countries by enhanced aid programs. As discussed in Chapter 2, aid is ineffective in some environments, but there are many low-income countries in which enhanced aid would raise growth and assist diversification away from dependence on primary commodities. Collier and Hoeffler (2000) simulate the effect of aid combined with economic policy reform in a poor, marginalized economy. Contrary to some suggestions, they find that neither aid nor policy reform are themselves direct risk factors. Both contribute to peace indirectly by raising growth and inducing diversification. In turn, growth and diversification reduce the risk of conflict. They find that over a period of five years the risk of conflict could be substantially reduced by aid combined with policy reform.

Globalization and culture

GLOBALIZATION CAN BOTH INCREASE AND REDUCE CULTURAL diversity. It increases diversity as foreign cultures are introduced by the power of communications and marketing, and by immigration. It reduces diversity if a foreign culture displaces local culture. Both these effects can be problematic.

Globalization increases diversity

Globalization increases social diversity as foreign cultures enter a society and co-exist with local culture. People become aware of different lifestyles through trade. For example, as Russia has opened its economy, the Swedish retailer IKEA has introduced Scandinavian style to consumers in Moscow, but this has not driven out Russian style. People also become aware of different lifestyles through migration. In Britain, the chicken tikka introduced by South Asian immigrants has become the most popular fast food, but this has not driven out fish and chips.

Greater cultural and ethnic diversity can make a society more dynamic, but it can also create problems. In popular perception diverse societies find it harder to cooperate and are more prone to violent conflict. There is indeed evidence that within local communities—such as cities in the United States or school boards in Kenya—cooperation is more difficult if the community is multiethnic. Many relationships depend upon trust, and cultural diversity can make trust more difficult. Initially, research suggested that these adverse effects of diversity were sufficiently important to affect national economic performance (Easterly and Levine 1997). However, there are other effects of diversity that are advantageous for growth: a diverse society has a wider range of information and more dynamic business networks. Subsequent research has established that economic growth is not adversely affected by ethnic diversity as long as a country is democratic (Collier 2000, 2001). Diversity is generally detrimental only in the context of dictatorship: narrow, ethnically based dictatorships are inclined to sacrifice the common good of enhanced growth for their own group interest. Hence, the diversity of globalization goes hand-in-hand with the need for democratization.

Similarly, the expectation that diversity increases violent conflict is not borne out by research. Controlling for other characteristics, societies that are highly diverse in terms of ethnicity and religion actually have a lower risk of large-scale violent conflict than homogeneous societies (Collier and Hoeffler 2001). The risk of violent conflict is somewhat higher if the society has one ethnic group in a majority, facing minority groups, but even this effect is quite small relative to other risk factors such as poverty.

Globalization reduces diversity

Cultures differ, and the members of a culture have a strong interest in passing their own culture on to the next generation. For example, Bisin and Verdier (2000) describe the considerable efforts that ethnic minorities devote to the inter-generational transmission of culture. Globalization can threaten this transmission, exposing youth to different cultures through the spread of ideas, goods and advertising, and through the movement of peoples. However, Bisin and Verdier find that cultures are remarkably resilient. Cultural transmission can withstand diversity, co-existing with other cultures in the same society. Obviously, what it cannot withstand is a situation in which imported culture is so powerful as to displace local culture. There are well-based fears that globalization will weaken the inter-generational transmission of culture as a result of displacement effects.

The most likely displacement effects may be for local culture to be displaced by western culture, and in particular by American culture. American films and brands have a large presence in the world economy. Both developing and developed countries see a danger of cultural homogenization and consequent loss of identity. The perception of the danger is real and strongly felt. Some countries subsidize their film and culture industries, which is permitted under WTO exceptions for products with a high cultural content. But there is no simple answer to this concern, and it is clearly a factor in countries' decision-making concerning integration with the global economy.

Globalization and the environment

Globalization and pollution

In previous chapters we have suggested that globalization raises incomes in most of the world and intensifies competition. The higher consumption that this enables poses a potential threat of environmental pollution. The intensification of competition also creates a potential for a "race to the bottom" and "pollution havens." Governments may try to attain a competitive advantage by lowering their environmental standards: the beggar-thy-neighbor problem of protectionism may be replaced by a beggar-thyself problem of globalization. Offsetting these effects, as incomes rise through globalization, people can afford to give greater priority to environmental quality. The net effect is likely to differ between countries. Some of the poorest countries may opt to become pollution havens. The new globalizers, where industrialization is most rapid but incomes are still low, may face environmental deterioration. The rich countries may opt to improve their environments. We now consider some of the evidence for these effects.

First, consider the ambiguous net effect of rising income. Some research has suggested that there is an environmental "Kuznets curve"— development initially worsens the environment, but eventually improves it again. If so, this implies both that development threatens the environment and that something can be done—and usually is done—to rectify it. There are quite good theoretical reasons to expect such a relationship, but the empirical evidence for it is mixed. The theoretical underpinnings cover political economy, technology, and economics. As incomes rise, concern for the environment increases and this induces a policy response that improves the environment (Grossman 1995). If pollution abatement technology exhibits increasing returns to scale, growth of the economy makes such technologies more accessible (Andreoni and Levinson 1998). For those natural resources that are traded, scarcity will itself inhibit degradation (Unruh and Moomaw 1998), while structural change in the economy favors service sectors that are less polluting than industry (Syrquin 1989). The empirical evidence is contested. A recent survey concludes that there is no evidence for a Kuznets curve *in general* (Borghesi 1999). However, for particular aspects of the environment the evidence is sometimes stronger. For air quality there is a strong Kuznets curve, although the actual turning point at which quality starts to improve is unclear (Cole, Rayner, and Bates 1997; Harbaugh, Levinson, and Wilson 2000). On water quality there is also some evidence for a Kuznets effect. For most other environmental indicators there is no such evidence. Even where there is an apparent Kuznets effect, most of the evidence comes from cross-section analysis of countries. What might be happening is that there are two separate processes going on simultaneously: environmental deterioration in developing countries and environmental improvement in rich countries, rather than these being two observations on a single trajectory. The evidence is more difficult to interpret because there are so few middle-income countries at what might be the turning point. Studies of countries that might be expected to be around the turning point find no evidence for it. For example, a study of Malaysia finds only continuing environmental degradation (Vincent 1997).

The evidence certainly does not support the complacent notion that environmental degradation is simply a temporary phase that can be easily reversed. On the contrary, degradation tends to accumulate over time and can become much more costly to reverse; indeed, if the costs of abatement become too high, environmental degradation becomes in an economic sense irreversible. Hence, a development policy that puts a priority on growth at the expense of the environment may be short-sighted, incurring avoidably high future costs.

Now consider the effect of intensifying competition. Environmental pollution can be limited through effective regulation. In turn, effective regulation requires effective state action: regulations must be devised and enforced by public agencies. Regulation is thus both a political and a bureaucratic process. Potentially, the intensification of competition can interfere with it as governments seek a competitive advantage for their country by imposing lower standards than other countries. This could show up both as a general race to lower standards and as pollution havens—the countries with the fewest other locational advantages aggressively abandoning all standards.

While there is no dispute that in theory intensified competition could give rise to pollution havens, the empirical evidence suggests that it has not happened on a significant scale. The main reason is that the costs imposed by environmental regulation are small relative to other considerations, and so their impact upon location decisions between rich and poor countries is minimal. As discussed in Chapter 1, there are large cost differences between locations due to factors such as transport, infrastructure and economic policy. By contrast, the cost of making a plant less polluting is usually remarkably cheap.

During third wave globalization, the new globalizers have indeed increased their share of global industrial production. This has increased their share of pollution intensive industries (Mani and Wheeler 1998). However, this increased production of pollution-intensive goods was not related to exporting: it largely met domestic demand. Developing countries harnessed their comparative advantage in *labor*-intensive industries, not in *pollution*-intensive industries. They have not increased their share of global pollution-intensive industrial exports. Indeed, their exports to rich countries are less pollution-intensive than their imports. The rich countries have actually strengthened their comparative advantage in pollution-intensive industries despite stricter environmental standards (Sorsa 1994; Mani and Wheeler 1998; Albrecht 1998). As we will see, developing countries do face severe problems of industrial pollution, but not as a result of pollution haven effects. Indeed, foreign-owned plants in developing countries, precisely the ones that according to the theory would be most attracted by low standards, tend to be less polluting than indigenous plants in the same industry. Most multinational companies adopt near-uniform standards globally, often well above the local government-set standards (Dowell, Hart, and Yeung 2000; Schot and Fischer 1993). This suggests that they relocate plants to developing countries for reasons other than low environmental standards. Paradoxically, the pollution haven effect may be more important within the national boundaries of a developed country than between rich and poor countries. Within a national boundary many of the other locational factors are less important, and so local environmental regulations might matter more. For example, there is evidence that regulations do affect locational decisions within the United States (Becker and Henderson 1997; Henderson 1996).

Similarly, there is little evidence for a race to the bottom—a competitive lowering of standards. New theoretical research suggests that this would manifest itself most strongly in the new globalizing economies (Chau and Kanbur 2001). However, two empirical studies do not find that countries have lowered their standards to attract foreign investment or to increase exports (Wheeler 2001; Jaffe and others 1995). Wheeler analyzes data on air quality in the industrial heartlands of three major new globalizing countries: Brazil, China, and Mexico. He finds that far from experiencing a race to the bottom, all three have registered improvements in air quality.

However, developing countries—both the more globalized and less globalized areas—do face major problems in developing effective environmental regulation. For example, a recent study of China shows that current environmental regulations are *far* weaker than would be justified if the social costs of abatement were properly balanced against the social benefits (Wang and Wheeler 1996). Such regulation requires both political and bureaucratic action. In many countries business lobbies can oppose the tightening of standards on the spurious grounds that this would impair their competitiveness. This process, known as "regulatory chill," is much more plausible than a competitive lowering of standards. The new globalizers need to raise their regulatory standards quickly as they rapidly industrialize, and this sort of lobbying can slow the process down. In addition to regulatory chill—which affects the political process—satisfactory environmental standards are impaired by weak bureaucracies. Some states have only limited capability for effective bureaucratic action. They lack the necessary revenue and skill base. Failing states will have poor enforcement of environmental standards regardless of their regulations. They are most unlikely to become international havens for polluting industries because virtually all industry needs supporting services that failing states cannot provide. However, local industry will be far more environmentally damaging than would be socially desirable. Where pollution has become particularly serious it sometimes provokes effective popular pressure. For example, in the Mexican city of Ciudad Guars smoke emissions from small brick kilns provoked widespread public pressure that induced politicians to act. In Indonesia environmental standards are effectively enforced by the simple strategy of grading firms according to their compliance and publicizing the results. More generally, the effectiveness of pollution control depends on the combination of a bureaucratic capability to measure pollutants and a political capability to act on the information. Democratic and participatory arrangements make it more likely that information will be used and can also make it more likely that it is collected. Countries differ markedly in the receptivity of the political process to the concerns of ordinary people, and this, rather than an environmental Kuznets curve, may account for the differing environmental paths. Many countries are simply not implementing pollution abatement measures that are readily available, cheap, and effective.

Globalization and deforestation

Official figures from the U.N. Food and Agriculture Organization (FAO) suggest that tropical regions are experiencing deforestation at a rate of about 0.7 percent per year and that this is accelerating. Such severe deforestation has several adverse consequences: the loss of a sustainable supply of forest products, hydrological impacts such as flooding, reduced biodiversity, and an increase in net greenhouse gas emissions.

Models of deforestation find that both growth and economic liberalization can accelerate deforestation (Angelsen and Kaimowitz 1999). Growth is associated with the encroachment of agriculture, and liberalization is associated with commercial logging, the two main causes of deforestation. However, establishing the effect of development on forest cover poses similar problems to its effect on environmental pollution. The global time series data are doubtful: for example, the FAO uses a model to estimate forest loss in which it is assumed that increased population density causes deforestation (Rudel and Roper 1997). However, the anthropological evidence challenges precisely this relationship. In a study of long term environmental change in Machakos, Kenya, Tiffen (1993) found that increased population density had actually reduced environmental degradation as open access resources were transformed into rule-managed regimes. Fairhead and Leach (1998) find a similar pattern in six West African countries. They conclude that official estimates of deforestation for these countries during the 20th century are between three and five times too high. Just because a natural resource becomes more valuable does not necessarily imply that it will become exploited in an unsustainable fashion. The response of Machakos farmers is an instance of a general phenomenon, the incentive to create regulated management.

While the extent of the global problem is thus contested, there are undeniably high rates of deforestation in some countries. Currently, the highest annual rates of tropical deforestation appear to be in the Philippines (3.5 percent), Sierra Leone (3 percent), and Thailand (2.6 percent). These disturbingly high rates may not be the direct result of the global market, but rather a particular interaction between it and local institutions. Ross (2001) provides an insightful analysis of deforestation in Thailand, one of the new globalizers. He shows how, as timber became more valuable, state officials themselves actively undermined the institutions that had been effectively regulating the industry. By undermining the institutions they were able to create opportunities for corruption—a process he terms "rent seizing." While in Thailand the dismantling of forestry regulation occurred in the context of overall development, deforestation in Sierra Leone occurred in a context of generalized state failure. As discussed above, this failure was in part attributable to the unregulated extraction of diamonds by rebel groups. Both cases suggest that local institutions can be undermined by the presence of valuable natural resources, although the effect is not inevitable: local actors also have an incentive to build institutions to regulate valuable resources, and the effect of international trade itself may be quite modest.

Although trade flows in tropical timber are relatively small (see box 4.2), there have been proposals to impose quotas or bans to counteract deforestation (see box 4.3). However, such efforts are unlikely to be successful unless they are part of an international mechanism by which countries are compensated for maintaining forests' global services for biodiversity and carbon sequestration. Domestic improvement of institutions is more likely to be effective where most production is for the domestic market, where the problems associated with deforestation are domestic, and where the policy failures are also domestic.

Box 4.2 Trade in tropical timber

A CLOSER LOOK AT THE INTERNATIONAL MARKET in tropical timber (industrial roundwood, sawnwood, wood-based panels, woodpulp, and paper products) shows that both export and import markets are largely dominated by developed countries. The principal exporters of forest products are North America and Western Europe, which in 1996 exported 35 percent and 39 percent of the world's industrial forest products, respectively (FAO 1999). The export share of developing countries varies considerably across commodity groups, with focus on industrial roundwood and wood-based panels (FAO 1999). Developing countries' share of total imports is the same as their export share, and relatively minor, with 22 percent of total world imports in 1996 (FAO 1999). As regards exports as a share of total production in 1996, developing countries exported 7 percent of their roundwood, 10 percent of sawnwood, and 39 percent of wood-based panels. The rest was consumed locally (FAO 1999).

The relatively small share of tropical timber in international trade flows prompted Sedja and Simpson's (1999) result that further trade liberalization in wood products would have only very modest

impact on deforestation. Panday and Wheeler (2000) analyze the effect of structural adjustment policies on wood products in 112 developing countries from 1961 to 1998. They find that although adjustment had strong impacts on imports, exports, production, and consumption of wood products, the net impact on domestic roundwood production (as a proxy for forest exploitation) has been close to zero. However, if trade liberalization leads to higher prices for tropical timber, deforestation may increase as logging becomes more profitable (Von Amsberg 1994, Barbier and others 1995, Deacon 1995). Furthermore, there is also an indirect effect of timber logging, apart from the removal of trees and other damage incurred to surrounding forest during timber extraction. Opening up and improving access to the forests facilitates agricultural conversion and fuelwood collection. Thus, the total effect of timber logging is likely to be understated by the contribution of wood extraction to deforestation. For the Philippines, Boyd, Hyde, and Krotilla (1991) find that tariff reduction for timber products would exacerbate deforestation. However, the main reasons are policy failures in the forestry sector and poor timber management.

Environmental regulation thus requires substantially more effort and resources than simple, targeted control of a few pollutants. Whether regulatory development can keep pace with economic development depends on whether environmental regulatory institutions can develop faster than public institutions more generally. The evidence is sparse, but the World Bank's own indicators of institutional and policy development provide some grounds for optimism (Wheeler 2000). Even general policy indicators are not closely correlated with economic development; they exhibit great variation at each income level. Further, environmental policy is sometimes far in advance of general policy, for example, in Belize, Bhutan, Ecuador, the Maldives, and the Seychelles. These are all countries where specific natural resources are important determinants of

---

Box 4.3   The use of trade instruments to address environmental issues is not the best sustainable approach

ALTHOUGH TRADE FLOWS IN TROPICAL TIMBER trade are small, and timber extraction is not a major source of deforestation, trade restrictions on timber have been proposed to address the global environmental aspects of deforestation. Such restrictions would be imposed on resource-based commodities exported by countries hosting threatened biodiversity, and imported by countries that are recipients of global biodiversity benefits. The Convention on International Trade in Endangered Species (CITES) is an example of an international agreement in the form of a ban on trade in selective endangered species, including some timber. Proposals for further trade bans in tropical timber have been advanced by timber-importing countries. Local governments in Germany and the Netherlands have implemented bans on the use of tropical timber. Product labeling has been implemented in Austria. The Netherlands has adopted a policy of importing only sustainably managed tropical timber since 1995 (Barbier and others 1994; Government of the Netherlands 1991). And the EU Parliament has brought forward a proposal to impose annual quotas on imports of tropical hardwood (Dean 1995).

The existing CITES ban is controversial, both politically and conceptually. Bulte and Kooten (1999) conclude that it arrested the decline of the African elephant population, and that continued trade and poaching could have driven the species to extinction. However, some African countries are now hosting growing elephant herds and criticize the convention because it prevents them from benefiting from their sustainable population management by exporting ivory.

Many experts (Barbier and others 1994; Swanson 1995) disapprove of trade bans like CITES: they are difficult to enforce (especially over the long run), create huge profits from illegal trade, and provide little incentive for host countries to implement sustainable resource management. There are similar reservations regarding a ban on tropical timber.

---

tourist revenue. In such cases even countries with low overall policy ratings have proven capable of focused efforts to protect critical environmental assets (Wheeler 2000). This reinforces the conclusion that even poorly administered societies can strengthen regulation when environmental damage is clear, costly, and concentrated in a few sites.

Global warming and other transnational environmental problems

In general, environmental problems (whether pollution or illegal trade in biodiversity) become harder to control when their effects are widespread and cross jurisdictional boundaries. Local public goods can often be regulated effectively by policymakers in individual countries. Regional and global public goods often require international coordination and treaties. Already, more than 200 multilateral environmental agreements (MEAs) have been concluded. The result is a form of environmental globalization—a growing international structure for environmental management reflecting the diversity of the issues and interests involved. Few of these MEAs regulate trade or contain trade provisions. Box 4.4 summarizes those that are of significance to the relationship between the environment and trade.

In general, trade restrictions are not the best option to protect the environment. Measures should be designed to affect the primary source of the problem in production, consumption, or waste disposal, regardless of whether the product is internationally traded. When one country's production or consumption decisions impose environmental

---

Box 4.4 Multilateral environmental agreements with trade provisions

CONVENTION ON INTERNATIONAL TRADE IN **Endangered Species (CITES).** Bans commercial international trade in an agreed list of endangered species. It also regulates and monitors (by use of permits, quotas, and other restrictive measures) trade in other species that might become endangered.

Montreal Protocol on Substances that Deplete the Stratospheric Ozone Layer. Lists certain substances as ozone depleting and bans all trade in those substances between parties and non-parties. Similar bans may be implemented against parties as part of the protocol's non-compliance procedure. The protocol also contemplates allowing import bans on products made with, but not containing, ozone-depleting substances—a ban based on process and production methods.

Basel Convention on the Control of Transboundary Movement of Hazardous Wastes and Their Disposal. Allows parties only to export a hazardous waste to another party that has not banned its import and that consents to the import in writing. Parties may not import from or export to a non-party. They are also obliged to prevent the import or export of hazardous wastes if they have reason to

believe that the wastes will not be treated in an environmentally sound manner at their destination.

Rotterdam Convention on the Prior Informed Consent Procedure for Certain Hazardous Chemicals and Pesticides in International Trade (PIC). From the convention's agreed list of chemicals and pesticides, parties can decide which ones they cannot manage safely and, therefore, will not import. When trade in the controlled substances does take place, labeling and information requirements must be followed. Decisions made by the parties must be trade neutral: if a party decides not to consent to imports of a specific chemical, it must also stop domestic production of the chemical for domestic use, as well as imports from any non-party.

Cartagena Protocol on Biosafety. Restricts import of some living genetically modified organisms as part of a carefully specified risk management procedure, as parties determine. Living GMOs that will be intentionally released to the environment are subject to an advance informed agreement procedure, and those destined for use as food, feed, or processing must be accompanied by documents identifying them.

externalities on other countries, such as acid rain, global warming, and biodiversity destruction, MEAs should be established to tax the unwanted emissions or fund the installation of appropriate technology or institutions. Only if this approach is not feasible may there be a theoretical case for using trade policy. Markusen (1975) and Baumol and Oates (1975, 1988) demonstrated that, in the case of transboundary pollution, a tariff on a polluting good could improve welfare. Further, tariffs may discipline countries to join and abide by MEAs. Even when some countries causing the environmental problem do not join an MEA, tariffs could avoid an undermining of the agreement through so called "pollution leakage." However, such tariffs would have to be well crafted since a large body of evidence shows that developing country factories exhibit great diversity in environmental performance (Wheeler and others 1999). It would therefore be inefficient and counterproductive to impose tariffs equally on exports from all firms. A further problem with tariffs for environmental purposes is that they could be challenged under GATT/WTO regulations (see box 4.5). The potential conflict between multilateral trade rules and multilateral environmental protection is one of the most contentious issues between environmental activists and those favoring trade liberalization.

However, to force developing countries to adopt OECD-quality environmental standards through trade threats would be an abuse of power by the industrial countries. Tariffs would be a form of taxation on poor countries—aid in reverse. If rich countries want higher standards than poor countries would themselves choose, they should induce poor countries to adopt higher standards through positive incentives rather than coercion.

The case of ozone-depleting chemicals demonstrates that the international community can control transboundary pollution effectively when the damage is obvious and widespread, and financial resources are made available to finance pollution abatement by poorer countries. Effective control of chlorofluorocarbons (CFCs) under the Montreal Protocol (see box 4.4) has been greatly aided by the relative concentration of major CFC sources, the willingness of OECD governments to subsidize rapid conversion, and the availability of substitutes. Similar factors have promoted effective international action to remove lead from gasoline.

In more diffuse, long-run cases such as persistent organic pollutants (POPs) and greenhouse gases, however, the international community has not mobilized as effectively. International negotiations for POPs phaseout have begun, because developing country governments perceive clear risks

Box 4.5   The World Trade Organization and multilateral environmental agreements

DO GATT/WTO RULES PREVENT ENVIRONMENTAL protection? This question is one of the key issues in the relationship between trade and environment.

According to its charter, the WTO strives for "the optimal use of the world's resources in accordance with the objective of sustainable development," and says that "members do not want to intervene in national or international environmental policies." Environmental advocacy groups have a different view. Greenpeace argues that the "application of the WTO rules is interfering with the ability of governments to respond to citizen demands for protection against threats to environment and health." And they conclude that "WTO policies fail to acknowledge that the…ecosystem imposed fixed limits on the amount of resources human beings can consume…without creating…an ecological catastrophe." At the heart of the debate is the potential conflict of trade measures in MEAs and GATT/WTO rules.

WTO and MEAs: So far, no dispute has arisen between WTO rules and trade measures in MEAs. However, several of the trade measures could potentially lead to violations of the central GATT/WTO

rule of non-discrimination between members. If a GATT/WTO member follows rules of an MEA to which it is party and applies trade restrictions against another GATT/WTO member that is not party to the MEA, but not against those GATT/WTO members who have signed the MEA, the rule of non-discrimination would be violated.

The WTO recognizes the potential conflict, but takes the view that problems are unlikely to arise. In the event of a conflict, the WTO considers its dispute settlement provisions satisfactory to tackle any problem.

Environmental NGOs, however, fear that in case of a clash free trade may prevail over environmental protection. The World Wildlife Fund thus advocates a reform of the WTO to "fully respect the authority and rules of international conservation and environmental agreements" and to "clearly recognize the limits of its jurisdiction over environmental questions." Greenpeace similarly demands that the WTO "ensure that its rules and decisions support rather than interfere with the objectives and effective implementation of MEAs."

for their own populations (Thornton 2000). As regards efforts to control greenhouse gases, a number of factors have so far prevented effective abatement. Environmental damage will accrue mostly in poor countries, is uncertain, and probably will take place well in the future. At the same time, the costs of reducing greenhouse gases will fall mainly on rich countries, are high, and must be paid now. If one looks at the seven largest emitters (accounting for 70 percent of CO_2 emissions) there are large differences in per capita emissions in rich countries such as the United States compared to poor countries such as India (figure 4.1).

The Kyoto protocol approach to greenhouse gasses is for rich countries to set themselves targets for emissions reduction, which is a positive step. The Global Commons Institute, an NGO, has come up with an innova-

Figure 4.1   Per capita CO$_2$ emissions in the E-7 economies, 1998

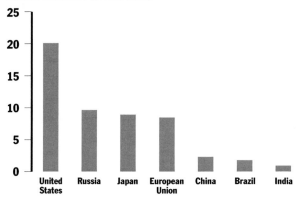

Source: Kraus and Shalizi (2001).

tive proposal that could extend participation in emissions reduction beyond the present signatories. The proposal entails agreeing on a target level of emissions by the year 2015 and then allocating these emissions to everyone in the world proportionally. Rich countries would get allocations well below their current level of emissions, while poor countries would get allocations well above. There would then be a market for emission permits. Poor countries could earn income selling some of their permits; rich and poor countries alike would have strong incentives to put energy-saving policies into place; and private industry would have strong incentives to invent new, cleaner technologies.

Similar international cooperative action has been favored by experts in view of the global environmental services from forests, both for preserving biodiversity and for carbon sequestration. Any agreement would have to find a mechanism to internalize positive externalities by paying for global forest services (Nordstroem and Vaughan 1999; Barbier 2000). This could be done either by relying on new markets for environmental services, such as joint implementation, bioprospecting deals, debt-for-nature swaps, or by establishing a global environmental organization that would ensure that host countries receive international compensation for additional conservation efforts that protect or provide global environmental benefits (Barbier 2000). So far, however, the convention on biological diversity and the international forest agreement have not received full international support.

Summary of recommendations

ONE OF THE DISTINCTIVE FEATURES OF THE THIRD WAVE of globalization is that the importance of developing countries in the world economy is growing. As this process occurs, it will be natural and desirable for this growing presence to be reflected in the power relations within international institutions such as the WTO, U.N. Security Council, World Bank, and IMF. The situation of each of these institutions is different, but the general point is that an increasing amount of economic interaction will be taking place outside of the OECD, so it is important that the new players in the world economy have substantial say in the architecture governing these interactions.

Globalization does limit the independence of national governments in some dimensions, but governments have many degrees of freedom to manage the interaction between trade, capital, and labor flows, on the one hand, and national culture and environment, on the other. Trade in cultural products should retain the special exemptions that they have within WTO rules. Many countries subsidize cultural products and cultural preservation in different ways, and globalization is consistent with the maintenance of a vibrant culture.

Similarly, many countries and communities are improving environmental conditions as globalization proceeds. Make no mistake: rapid industrialization in the new globalizers will increase pollution unless checked by improved regulation. There is great variation in environmental conditions in developing and developed countries, including among successful globalizers. Thus, it is possible to protect the environment through local collective action, but many locations are not doing it.

Global warming requires international collective action. There are many ways of achieving effective restraint. The Kyoto protocol approach is for rich countries to set themselves targets for emissions reductions, and the recent agreement between European nations and Japan to move ahead with the protocol is a positive step forward. Looking further down the road, it is critically important to get at least all of the E-7 involved. The Global Commons Institute, an NGO, has come up with an innovative proposal for how to do this. The proposal entails agreeing on a target level of emissions by the year 2015 and then allocating these emissions to everyone in the world proportionally. Rich countries would get allocations well below their current level of emissions, while poor countries would get allocations well above. There would then be a market for emission permits. Poor countries could earn income selling some of their permits; rich and poor countries alike would have strong incentives to put energy-saving policies into place; and private industry would have strong incentives to invent new, cleaner technologies. One of the hopeful things about globalization is how an innovative idea like this can quickly gain currency and support.

CHAPTER FIVE

An Agenda for Action

S INCE 1980 THE WORLD HAS INTEGRATED AS NEVER before: poor countries with some 3 billion people have broken into global industrial markets. As poor people in these countries get jobs, the tide of poverty and inequality that had previously engulfed the world is starting to turn. So far, this process is fragile. Some 2 billion people live in countries that have been left out of globalization. Action is needed to reinforce and secure what could become a historic turning point.

As the world has integrated, for the first time in history civil society has become able to conduct a global discourse. This has created the potential, and the urgent need, for global collective action. There is a backlog of problems needing global action, and globalization itself has created problems as well as prosperity. Developing countries have divided into more globalized ones, where poverty is rapidly diminishing, and less globalized ones, where poverty is rising. The rapid growth of the new globalizers is generating profound changes in their societies and is challenging rich countries in some markets. The absolute decline of many marginalized countries is a tragedy for both them and the world. An integrated world can neither tolerate nor withstand the exclusion of 2 billion people from the prospect of prosperity.

Concern about globalization is itself a global phenomenon. Our report has highlighted many of the anxieties that people have about globalization. Most are grounded in reality. The objective of our research is to examine the effects of different aspects of integration, with two main aims in mind: helping countries to find policies that reduce and mitigate the costs and risks of integration, and helping them to assess tradeoffs so they can make well-informed choices. Our point of departure is that many poor countries have chosen to become more integrated with the global economy. Research can help them design policies for this integration and inform their policy debates. In this concluding chapter we pull together our discussion.

In the next section we organize our findings around the various anxieties about globalization. Although the world in integrating, it is deeply divided: many anxieties stem from the particular experiences of various countries. We take in turn the anxieties of the countries that are less globalized, the anxieties of the new globalizers, and those of the rich countries. We conclude with those concerns that are truly global. Sometimes people are worrying about the right things, sometimes about the wrong things. Some of the adverse effects of globalization have not received sufficient attention, while some of the imagined adverse effects turn out not to be major problems.

In the final section we propose an agenda for action. Although globalization has created problems, it has also been the engine of remarkable poverty reduction among the 3 billion people of the new globalizing countries. Actions that simply reverse globalization would come at an intolerably high price, destroying the prospects of prosperity for many millions of poor people. There are less divisive, less cavalier ways of meeting well-founded concerns. Some policy changes will require global action. Others depend on the specific actions of governments in developing countries and rich counties. Bringing about these policy changes will require popular pressure not just for global action, but for national action.

Anxieties and their foundation

Anxieties of the less globalized countries

Some two billion people live in countries that are not integrating strongly in the global economy. They are dependent on a narrow range of primary commodity exports and on average are in absolute economic decline.

Continued economic marginalization. The core anxiety of many countries is that they will be marginalized, failing to penetrate global industrial markets even if they change policies. For many of these countries this anxiety is likely to be misplaced, but only if policy and institutional change are substantial and thought through locally so that it is appropriate for local circumstances. Simply liberalizing trade policy will not usually be sufficient for success in global markets. The entire investment climate must be improved, from infrastructure through to the supporting institutions.

For some countries, however, continued marginalization will be the harsh reality. Some countries are so disadvantaged by location that they probably have little realistic prospect of developing. Which countries fall into this category is uncertain: economists' record of forecasting failure is not impressive. Nobel prize winner James Meade forecast in the 1950s that Mauritius was doomed to dependence on sugar: in the 1970s it became one of the world's fastest growing countries by penetrating the global garments market. Nobel winner Gunnar Myrdal forecast in the 1960s that Indonesia would not develop: in the 1980s it began dramatic reductions in poverty, aided by labor-intensive manufactured exports. While it is therefore unwise to write countries off, it would be equally foolish to imagine that all countries will industrialize. For the countries that do not industrialize, the global challenge is to aid alternative development strategies and to permit migration to other areas.

The failure of the state. Some governments in marginalized countries face real anxieties about their physical control of their own territory. Poverty, dependence on primary commodity exports, and economic decline are all significant risk factors in violent internal conflict. More broadly, the state often lacks the capacity for effective delivery of public services and for regulation of the environment. Social outcomes can deteriorate as a result, as they have in much of Africa. Conflict, poverty, and a lack of human development feed on each other, like a trap.

Anxieties of the new globalizers

Some 3 billion people live in countries that have recently succeeded in penetrating global industrial markets. Their economies are in the early stages of rapid growth that is already bringing down poverty. This growth is probably dependent on continued access to OECD markets. Rapid economic growth brings social and environmental disruption, challenging both the government and civil society to provide new forms of social and environmental protection.

Being shut out of markets. One of the main anxieties of policymakers in the new globalizing countries is that they will be shut out of rich country markets. These leaders have been encouraged for a long time to open up their economies, and now that many developing countries have moved on this agenda there is real concern about rising protectionism in rich countries. Overall rich country trade policies are relatively open, but sectors where they maintain protection are precisely those in which the new globalizers have comparative advantage. Developing countries confront European agricultural subsidies, U.S. anti-dumping actions, foot dragging over the phaseout of the multifiber agreement governing textile trade, and high tariffs on selected products produced by developing countries.

Part of this fear of being shut out of markets relates to the growing trend to add institutional requirements to trade agreements. Efforts to impose labor and environmental regulations through trade sanctions could become new forms of protectionism.

Being subject to the whims of distant investors. Many of the new globalizers have opened up for foreign investment at the same time that they have liberalized trade. It makes sense that these policies go together. Much of the manufactures and services trade in today's world is related to production networks and MNCs. The developing countries that have seen large increases in imports and exports are by and large the same ones that have received the largest flows of FDI. The entry of MNCs does not inevitably weaken governments. As the new globalizers grow, the size of their government sector should usually grow both absolutely and relative to the rest of the economy. The share of government expenditure in GDP is only 20 percent in low- and middle-income countries, versus 30–50 percent in richer countries.

One of the deepest fears in the developing world is of financial and exchange rate crises that have huge costs. Such fears are sensible. Even with sound fundamentals, financially open economies can be hit by contagion effects of crises starting elsewhere. As in domestic markets, international financial markets can be beset by irrational booms and crashes. We have emphasized that full financial opening must be approached cautiously. We agree with the strategy of such countries as China and India to allow FDI while maintaining capital controls on other flows. Also, some of that FDI can be into the banking sector, helping to strengthen the domestic financial infrastructure. Allowing foreign banks to provide services is different from opening the capital account, although as FDI, including in financial services, proceeds, it probably becomes more difficult to isolate an economy from the international financial market. Good fundamentals alone are not sufficient to insulate countries from financial crises, but they certainly help.

Being uncompetitive. The new globalizers fear being uncompetitive. The typical developing country must compete with the big corporations from the rich countries, the established emerging markets such as Korea, and the big newcomers, especially China. The firm-level evidence shows clearly that opening up is likely to lead to the closure of some plants, and there will be more turnover in an open economy. However, there will also be more entry—plants of foreign firms and domestic entrepreneurs will start up in response to new opportunities. Firms and locations in the developing world can be competitive. There are many successful examples.

Clearly an important agenda for the new globalizers is continued improvement in the investment climate. This involves the regulatory framework for starting and closing firms and for hiring and firing workers. It also involves infrastructure (financial services, telecommunications, ports, and power) and economic governance (contract enforcement, fair taxation, and control of corruption). We have emphasized that developing countries can use FDI and the international market for services to improve elements of the investment climate. Many countries have benefited from foreign investment in banking, telecommunications, and power.

Trading good jobs for bad ones. The importance of creating a good climate for firms naturally raises fears that globalization works against workers and will lead to heightened inequality in developing countries. The evidence shows that this is not the case. Trade liberalization, FDI, and out-migration of unskilled workers have all been found to raise wages in the South. More generally, the developing countries participating strongly in globalization have seen large increases in per capita income, with the benefits widely diffused. The result has been rapid reductions in poverty. For poor countries, integration has not resulted in a "race to the bottom" in wages and labor standards. To the contrary, incomes and wages have risen, and along with them have come improvements in labor standards. Raising family income is the most effective way to reduce abusive child labor.

While integration raises wages on average and for many specific occupations, there will inevitably be some losers from globalization. Capitalists and workers in protected industries are the most visible losers, which is why they are a vocal force for protection in all countries. We also noted that in an open economy there will be more turnover of firms, creating temporary unemployment and hardship. Finally, there is a tendency for opening up to raise the return to education. This more dynamic environment calls for new types of social protection. To get reforms underway may require one-time compensation schemes for workers who would otherwise suffer large losses. Well-designed unemployment insurance and severance pay systems can provide protection to formal sector workers in an environment that will now have more entry and exit of firms. But the poorest people are better reached through self-targeting programs such as food-for-work schemes. Finally, and perhaps most important, the combination of openness and a well-educated labor force produces especially good results for poverty reduction and human welfare. Hence, a good education system that provides opportunities for all is critical for success in this globalizing world.

Environmental degradation. The rapid industrialization taking place in the new globalizers can substantially increase pollution and depletion of natural resources. However, this is not inevitable; for example, air quality in many globalizing cities has been rising. The outcome depends on the ability to develop effective regulation. Far from environmental regulation being a luxury that can lag development, the necessary institutions must be developed more rapidly than general institutional development.

Social dislocation. As the new globalizers develop rapidly, they face massive internal migrations from rural areas to towns. Often adjoining countries are being marginalized, so there is also large-scale immigration. These influxes increase social and ethnic diversity and this in turn can make social cooperation more difficult. There is indeed evidence that ethnically diverse cities tend to have worse-performing public services. However, the research evidence suggests that these anxieties are greatly exaggerated. Diverse societies are not more prone to large-scale violence. Indeed, the rapid income growth of the new globalizers is making them safer societies. Despite the greater difficulties of cooperation, diverse societies have offsetting advantages. Overall economic performance is not adversely affected by diversity as long as societies are democratic.

International imbalances in power. During the Cold War some developing countries gained an international voice by playing the superpowers against each other. During the past decade the world has been more unipolar than at any time for at least a century. However, on present patterns of growth this phase will be short lived. Partly as a result of globalization, China and India are both growing far more rapidly than the OECD economies. Over the coming decades international economic power is likely to be multipolar, and this in turn can be expected gradually to reshape the architecture of international governance.

Rich country anxieties are somewhat different

There may well be more anxiety about globalization in rich countries than in poor ones. Certainly the nature of the fears and their foundations in reality are somewhat different.

Globalization and terrorism. Evidently, after the attack on the World Trade Center, one of the big fears in rich countries is that globalization has increased the risk of international terrorism. In an important sense this is correct: terrorist organizations have globalized more rapidly than have government efforts to counter them. Given the international structure of modern terrorism, isolated national efforts to counter it have become ineffective—anti-terrorism has become a global public good. As with other such goods, it has been woefully under-supplied. International terrorism has not only exploited the limitations of uncoordinated national efforts, it has also exploited the safe havens available in failed states. Development policy can play an important role in ending these safe havens. Economic weakness is a major cause of state failure; and economic recovery is integral to state reconstruction.

Globalization and inequality within rich countries. One of the biggest fears in rich countries is that globalization is leading to greater inequality. This fear has more foundation for rich countries than for poor ones. The evidence suggests that FDI from North to South and migration from South to North both raise wages in the South and reduce wages in the North, other things being equal. Thus, these aspects of integration can be equalizing in the South and disequalizing in the North.

The United States has seen a significant rise in inequality, and credible estimates suggest that migration has played a role in this, though skill-biased technological change and tax policy have also clearly played a role. The very large differences in inequality between equally globalized rich countries suggest that factors other than globalization are more important.

Globalization and the loss of manufacturing jobs to low-wage countries. Most developed countries have been shifting employment out of manufacturing during the third wave of globalization. Some of this is due to changes in technology—manufacturing has become less labor intensive—but some of it is undoubtedly due to the movement of manufacturing jobs to low-income countries.

This need not imply rising unemployment or falling manufacturing wages, but rather a shift from manufacturing to service jobs. High-wage manufacturing will not be wiped out. Manufacturing within the

151

high-income countries has an enormous competitive advantage due to its proximity to its major market. Far from modern technology eliminating these advantages, it might actually be increasing them. The new retail technologies pioneered by Wal-Mart, with information on market conditions passed to suppliers daily, create a premium on very rapid delivery to market. Manufacturing workers in rich countries will continue to earn much higher wages than their counterparts in the new globalizers, simply because they are in the right place.

Globalization and homogenization. If globalization forces everyone toward common institutions and policies, then Europe can expect the kind of developments that have occurred in the United States. The United States is the largest and in some respects the most successful economy on earth, generating opportunities for millions of poor people, many of them immigrants from developing countries, to rise to prosperity. But it is not the only model of success. Several European and Asian economies match or exceed the American level of income per capita while having radically different policies and more equal social outcomes. For example, Austria, Belgium, Denmark, Japan, and Norway are relatively open economies. All have far less inequality than the United States with similar average income. By combining prosperity with equity they are the closest the world has yet come to eradicating poverty. Voters in the United States and these countries have chosen substantially different models, both of which work given their respective histories.

Culturally, as societies integrate in many respects, they become more diverse: IKEA has brought Swedish design to Russians, co-existing with Russian design; Indian immigrants and McDonalds' have brought chicken tikka and hamburgers to Britain, co-existing with fish and chips. However, without policies to foster local and other cultural traditions, many fear globalization may indeed lead to a dominance of American culture.

Global anxieties

Mounting global inequality. A widespread view of globalization is that it "makes rich people richer and poor people poorer." This simply does not seem to be true: poverty is falling rapidly in those poor countries that are integrating into the global economy. As Amartya Sen has argued, a more accurate concern would be over the staggering *level* of global inequality rather than its change. In the century before 1980 world inequality increased enormously; since then it has stabilized and may be declining. The pre-industrial world was more equal but much poorer, and returning to such a world is neither realistic nor desirable. Rather, the benefits of modernization must be spread more widely. Since 1980 this has begun to happen: the new globalizers are catching up with the rich countries. Poverty is largely rural; people are seizing the opportunities provided by industrialization to migrate from rural poverty to the first rungs of the urban jobs ladder. But so far, countries with about 2 billion people have not participated strongly in gobalization and have been falling further behind.

This pattern of convergence for some poor countries and divergence for others can be changed. Many more poor countries can globalize and join the group that is converging on rich countries. However, it would be unrealistic to expect all poor countries to be able to integrate into global industrial production. Opening up to trade and investment will not do much for people in many of the locations that are stagnating and by itself cannot be the solution to poverty there. For some of the currently marginalized countries, the key problem is poor institutions and policies. In other cases there are severe geographic problems of disease and isolation. While opening up will not do much for these locations, it is also clear that closing themselves off from the world economy has not generated prosperity.

While economic globalization cannot do much to help these locations, social globalization—recognizing an affinity among people that does not stop at national borders—may have more potential. It can be the impetus for global solutions to problems of poor governance, health, and infrastructure.

Global warming. Economic development, spurred by globalization, creates new environmental problems that must be tackled at the global level. An important worldwide fear is that governments will not move effectively to limit greenhouse gas emissions and roll back global warming. There is broad agreement among scientists that human activity has led to global warming and that much greater climate change is in store unless collective, corrective actions are taken. Where the problem comes from is clear. Seven economies (the E-7) account for 70 percent of CO_2 emissions. The United States, with only 4 percent of the world's population, emits nearly 25 percent of greenhouse gases. China is the second largest emitter, followed by the EU, the Russian Federation, Japan, India, and Brazil. In per capita terms the United States (with 20 metric tons per capita) is far ahead of other economies in terms of CO_2 emissions. Per capita emissions in China, Brazil, and India lag far behind those of the developed countries, and these disparities must be taken into account in any global agreement to roll back the emissions that cause global warming.

Globalization and the power of governments, labor, and capital. As a country integrates into the global industrial economy the role of government does not diminish. Traditional functions such as education still must be carried out, and to a higher standard, while government takes on new functions such as social protection and environmental regulation. In some areas of policy—notably macroeconomic management—room for maneuver is reduced. However, governments retain a wide range of choice over distributional policies. Occasionally, governments compete with each other by offering subsidies to attract new plants in those industries characterized by agglomeration and large scale. This is wasteful; to avoid it governments are increasingly cooperating, setting rules that limit incentives.

Since workers find it very difficult to organize across national borders, firms can potentially reduce the bargaining power of nationally organized unions by operating in multiple clusters and threatening to relocate investment between clusters. This may gradually lead to wage convergence among manufacturing clusters within high-income countries, although quite large differences between labor costs in manufacturing have proved persistent.

The evidence that wages have risen so rapidly in the new globalizers suggests that labor is empowered by rapid growth more than it is threatened by the greater mobility of capital. The jobs that are shifted to low-income countries do not pay as much as those that are lost. Capital probably gains as a result of this shift: workers in low-income countries usually have less power in their relationship with management, although the main winners are the people who buy the cheaper manufactures. Although wage jobs in low-income countries pay less than those in high-income countries, they are usually much better relative to the average work available in the society. Most manufacturing workers in high-income countries are not well off relative to others in their society. By contrast, most manufacturing workers in low-income countries earn far above the national average income.

Globalization intensifies competition, and this actually weakens the market power of capital. There is clear evidence of a squeeze in price-cost margins, suggesting that the power of national monopolies and cartels has been reduced. However, the world currently lacks an adequate regulatory authority to address problems of global market power. As with global warming, this is an important example of problems outpacing global policy.

Building an inclusive world economy: An agenda for action

RECENT GLOBALIZATION HAS BEEN A FORCE FOR POVERTY reduction, and has helped some large poor countries to narrow the gap with rich countries. However, some of the widespread anxieties are well founded: globalization could be much more effective for poor people, and its adverse effects could be substantially reduced. In important respects global policies are not keeping pace with global opportunities and global risks. In our report we propose an agenda for action, both global and local, that could make globalization work better and help countries and people that have been marginalized. In part our agenda overlaps with the agenda of those who protest globalization, but it is diametrically opposed to the nationalism, protectionism, and anti-industrial romanticism that is all too prominent. Our study highlights many actions that could help make globalization more beneficial. Of these, we will emphasize seven that we see as particularly important for making globalization work for the poor.

Participation in an expanding global market has basically been a positive force for growth and poverty reduction in developing countries. There are, however, very significant barriers to trade and a *first* area for action is a "development round" of trade negotiations. A "development round" should focus first and foremost on market access. Rich countries maintain protection in exactly the areas where developing countries have comparative advantage, and there would be large gains to poor countries if these were reduced. Furthermore, developing countries would gain a lot from better access to each other's markets—barriers between them are still higher than those from developed countries. These improvements in access are best negotiated in a multilateral context.

Developing countries have a good argument that trade agreements should not impose labor or environmental standards on poor countries. Communities all over the world are struggling to improve living standards and labor and environmental conditions. There are positive ways that rich countries can support this. A real and positive commitment, however, requires real resources (more below on this). Imposing trade sanctions on countries that do not meet first world standards for labor and environmental conditions can have deeply damaging effects on the living standards of poor people and for that reason is unconstructive. Furthermore, there is all too much danger that trade sanctions to enforce these standards will become new forms of protectionism that make the poor worse off. The more general point here is that trade agreements should leave countries free to take different institutional approaches to environmental standards, social protection, cultural preservation, and other issues. Among globalized countries there is great diversity of institutions and cultures, and we see no reason why economic integration cannot respect that.

Our research shows that open trade and investment policies are not going to do much for poor countries if other policies are bad. The locations in the developing world that are prospering during this most recent wave of globalization are ones that have created reasonably good investment climates in which firms, particularly small domestic firms, can start up, prosper, and expand. Hence a *second* key area for action is improving the investment climate in developing countries. A sound investment climate is not one full of tax breaks and subsidies for firms. It is rather an environment of good economic governance—control of corruption, well-functioning bureaucracies and regulation, contract enforcement, and protection of property rights. Connectivity to other markets within a country and globally (through transport and telecommunications infrastructure) is a key part of a good investment climate. A bad investment climate hits agriculture and small firms even harder than bigger firms.

Developing a sound investment climate is primarily a national and local responsibility and should focus particularly on the problems facing small firms. Employment in the small and medium-sized firms in towns and rural areas will be central to raising the living standards of the rural poor. Communities can use foreign investment and the international market for services to strengthen the investment climate. The presence of foreign banks in the local market strengthens the financial infrastructure. With the right incentives, foreign investment can efficiently provide power, ports, telecommunications, and other business services.

The evidence is quite strong that integration with the global market raises the return to education in different types of countries (both rich and poor). The higher return to education can be a positive thing, as it encourages households to invest in their children. But this highlights the importance of good delivery of education and health services—the *third* element in our agenda. If poor people have little or no access to health and education services, then it is very hard for them to benefit from the growth spurred by integration. With poor social services, globalization can easily lead to mounting inequality within a country and persistence of extreme poverty. For the newly globalizing developing countries as a group, there has been impressive progress in educational attainment—especially for primary education—and decline in infant mortality, suggesting that many locations have made the complementary investments in social services that are critical to ensure that the poor benefit from growth. The combination of strong education for poor people and a more positive investment climate is critical for empowering poor people to participate in the benefits of a more strongly expanding economy. But empowerment goes much deeper than this. It is about organizing property rights and governance in a way that involves poor people in decisions that affect their lives.

While integration has on average been a positive force for growth and poverty reduction in developing countries, there are inevitably specific winners and losers, especially in the short run. This is true in rich and poor countries. The firm-level evidence shows that much of the dynamic benefit of open trade and investment comes from more "churning" of plants—less efficient ones die, and new ones start up and expand. With this comes more labor market churning as well—probably the key reason why globalization is so controversial. It raises wages on average in both rich and poor countries, but there are some significant losers. Thus, the *fourth* area for action is to provide social protection tailored to the more dynamic labor market in an open economy. This is important to help individual workers who will lose in the short run from opening up, as well as to create a solid social foundation on which households—especially poor ones—feel comfortable taking risks and showing entrepreneurship. We try to document what works in a relatively rich country, and for formal sector workers, and what works in poor countries and for the large number of poor in the informal sector and rural areas. If policymakers do not put workable social protection measures into place, then many individual people will be hurt and the whole integration undertaking becomes suspect.

The *fifth* component of our action program is a greater volume of foreign aid, better managed. Aid should be targeted to a number of different problems. The evidence shows that, when low-income countries reform and improve the investment climate and social services, private investment—both domestic and foreign—responds with a lag. It is precisely in this environment that large-scale aid can have a great impact on growth and poverty reduction. Thus, while creating a sound policy environment is primarily a national and local responsibility, the world can help societies making difficult changes with financial support. Supporting low-income reformers—both at the national level and at the local level—is a key role for aid. Another important role for aid is to address some of the specific health and geographic challenges of marginalized countries and people. We have emphasized that there are locations that face difficult geographic challenges and that policy reform alone is not going to do much in these places. More aid should be targeted to research into health and agricultural technologies that could make a large difference in locations suffering from malaria and other challenges. Beyond research, there is obviously a need for assistance to deliver these health innovations to those who would benefit from them.

Our *sixth* area for action is debt relief. This is a kind of aid, but we do not want our recommendation here to get lost in our more general call for greater aid. Many of the marginalized countries, especially in Africa, are burdened with unsustainable debts. Reducing the debt burdens of these countries will be one factor enabling them to participate more strongly in globalization. Debt relief is particularly powerful when combined with policy reform (improvements in the investment climate and social services). Debt relief should make a significant difference for countries that have reasonably sound policy environments for poverty reduction, as in the HIPC initiative. It is important to put debt relief in the larger context of the overall foreign aid for marginalized countries. Debt relief should not come out of the existing envelope for aid (in which case little of real value will result) but rather needs to be complemented with greater overall volumes of assistance.

The six areas that we have highlighted for policy action on globalization are primarily in the economic realm and aim to raise the income and living standards of poor people. However, our report also examines a wide range of non-economic issues—power, culture, environment—and presents evidence about the effect of globalization on these important issues. We highlight many specific actions that can mitigate the risks and costs of globalization. Here in the action program, the *seventh* measure to highlight is the importance of tackling greenhouse gases and global warming. There is broad agreement among scientists that human activity is leading to climate change and that disastrous global warming is in store unless collective, corrective action is taken. This is one example of a critical area in which there a lack of effective global cooperation at this point. It is also one of the global problems that is going to particularly burden poor countries and poor people if it is not addressed.

The falling costs of communications, information, and transport that have contributed to globalization will not be reversed, but the reduction in trade and investment barriers could be reversed by protectionism and nationalism—as happened in the 1930s. However, protectionism and nationalism would be a profoundly damaging reaction to the challenges created by globalization. The problems must be addressed, but they are manageable. The reasonable concerns about globalization can be met without sacrificing the potential for global economic integration to dramatically benefit poor countries and poor people. Many poor people are benefiting from globalization. The challenge is to bring more of them into this process, not to retreat to the insularity and nationalism of the 1930s.

References

The word "processed" describes informally reproduced works that may not be commonly available through library systems.

Abadie, Alberto, and Javier Gardeazabal. 2001. "The Economic Costs of Conflict: A Case Control Study for the Basque Country." Kennedy School of Government, Harvard University, Boston, MA. Processed.

Abreu, M. 1996. "Trade in Manufactures: The Outcome of the Uruguay Round and Developing Country Interests." In W. Martin and L. A. Winters, eds., *The Uruguay Round and the Developing Economies*. Cambridge, England; New York and Melbourne: Cambridge University Press.

Ades, A., and E. Glaeser. 1999. "Evidence on Growth, Increasing Returns, and the Extent of the Market." *Quarterly Journal of Economics* 114(3): 1025–46.

Aitken, B., and A. Harrison. 1999. "Do Domestic Firms Benefit from Foreign Direct Investment? Evidence from Venezuela." *American Economic Review* 89(3): 605–18.

Albrecht, J. 1998. "Environmental Policy and Inward Investment Position of U.S. Dirty Industries." *Intereconomics* 33(4): 186–94.

Anderson, K., J. Francois, T. Hertel, B. Hoekman, and W. Martin. 2000. "Potential Gains from Trade Reform in the New Millennium." World Bank, Washington, D.C. Processed.

Andreoni, J., and A. Levinson. 1998. "The Simple Analytics of the Environmental Kuznets Curve." National Bureau of Economic Research Working Paper no. 6739, National Bureau of Economic Research, Cambridge, MA.

Angelsen, A., and D. Kaimowitz. 1999. "Rethinking the Causes of Deforestation: Lessons from Economic Models." *The World Bank Observer* 14(1): 73–98.

Artecona, R., and W. Cunningham. 2001. "Effects of Trade Liberalization on the Gender Wage Gap in Mexico." World Bank, Washington D.C. Processed.

Aw, B. Y., S. Chung, and M. J. Roberts. 2000. "Productivity and the Decision to Export: Micro Evidence from Taiwan and South Korea." *World Bank Economic Review* 14(1): 65–90.

Barbier, E. (2000). "Biodiversity, Trade, and International Agreements." *Journal of Economic Studies* 27(1/2): 55–74.

Barbier, E., N. Bockstael, J. Burgess, and I. Strand. 1995. "The Linkages between Timber Trade and Tropical Deforestation: Indonesia." *The World Economy* 18(3): 411–42.

Barbier, E., J. Burgess, J. Bishop, and B. Aylward. 1994. *The Economics of the Tropical Timber Trade.* London, Great Britain: Earthscan.

Baumol, W., and W. Oates. 1975. *The Theory of Environmental Policy.* New York: Prentice Hall.

_____. 1988. *The Theory of Environmental Policy.* Second edition. New York: Cambridge University Press.

Becker, R., and V. Henderson. 1997. "Effects of Air Quality Regulation on Decisions of Firms in Polluting Industries." National Bureau of Economic Research Working Paper No. 6160, National Bureau of Economic Research, Cambridge, MA.

Behrman, J. R., N. Birdsall, and M. Székely. 2000. "Economic Reform and Wage Differentials in Latin America." Inter-American Development Bank Research Working Paper No. 435, Inter-American Development Bank, Washington, D.C.

Bell, L. 1997. "The Impact of Minimum Wages in Mexico and Colombia." *Journal of Labor Economics* 15(3): S102–S135.

Bernard, A., and B. Jensen. 1999. "Exceptional Exporter Performance: Cause, Effect, or Both?" *Journal of International Economics* 47(1): 1–25.

_____. 2001. "Who Dies? International Trade, Market Structure, and Industrial Restructuring." National Bureau of Economic Research Working Paper No. W8327, National Bureau of Economic Research, Cambridge, MA.

Beyer, H., P. Rojas, and R. Vergara. 1999. "Trade Liberalization and Wage Inequality." *Journal of Development Economics* 59(1): 103–23.

Bigsten, A., and others. 2000. "Exports and Firm Level Efficiency in African Manufacturing." Centre for the Study of African Economies. Working Paper Series 2000–16: 1–23, July 2000.

Bisin, A., and T. Verdier. 2000. "Beyond the Melting Pot: Cultural Transmission, Marriage, and the Evolution of Ethnic and Religious Traits." *Quarterly Journal of Economics* 115(3): 955–88.

Blackhurst, R., B. Lyakurwa, and A. Oyejide. 2001. "Options for Improving Africa's Participation in the WTO." In B. Hoekman and W. Martin, eds., *Developing Countries and the WTO: A Pro-Active Agenda.* Oxford, Great Britain: Blackwell.

Blomstrom, M., and A. Kokko. 1996. "The Impact of Foreign Investment on Host Countries: A Review of the Empirical Evidence." World Bank Policy Research Working Paper No. 1745, World Bank, Washington, D.C.

Bordo, M. D., B. Eichengreen, and D. A. Irwin. 1999. "Is Globalization Today Really Different than Globalization a Hundred Years Ago?" National Bureau of Economic Research Working Paper 7195, National Bureau of Economic Research, Cambridge, MA.

Bordo, M., B. Eichengreen, D. Klingebiel, and M. S. Martinez-Peria. 2001. "Is the Crisis Growing More Severe?" *Economic Policy* 31: 51–82.

Borghesi, S. 1999. "The Environmental Kuznets Curve: A Survey of the Literature." Fondazione Eni Enrico Mattei. Nota di Lavoro (Italy); 85.99:1–30.

Borjas, G. J., R. B. Freeman, and L. F. Katz. 1997. "How Much Do Immigration and Trade Affect Labor Market Outcomes." *Brookings Papers on Economic Activity* 1: 1–90.

Bourguignon, F., and C. Morrisson. 2001. "Inequality among World Citizens: 1820–1992." Working Paper 2001–25, DELTA, Paris.

Boyd, W., F. Hyde, and K. Krutilla. 1991. "Trade Policy and Environmental Accounting: A Case Study of Structural Adjustment and Deforestation in the Philippines." Department of Economics, Ohio State University, Columbus, OH.

Brito, D. L., and M. D. Intriligator. 1992. "Narcotraffic and Guerilla Warfare: A New Symbiosis." *Defense Economics* 3(4): 263–74.

Bulte, E., and V. C. Kooten. 1999. "Economic Efficiency, Resource Conservation, and the Ivory Trade Ban." *Ecological Economics* 28(2): 171–81.

Burnside, C., and D. Dollar. 2000. "Aid, Policies, and Growth." *The American Economic Review* 90(4): 847–68.

Burnside, C., M. Eichenbaum, and S. Rebelo. Forthcoming. "Prospective Deficits and the Asian Currency Crises." *Journal of Political Economy*.

Byrd, W., and Q. Lin, eds. 1990. *China's Rural Industry: Structure, Development, and Reform.* New York: Oxford University Press.

Cairncross, F. 1997. *The Death of Distance: How the Communications Revolution Will Change Our Lives.* Boston, MA: Harvard Business School Press.

Calvo, S., L. Leiderman, and C. Reinhart. 1996. "Inflows of Capital to Developing Countries in the 1990s." *Journal of Economic Perspectives* 10(2): 123–39.

Cannadine, David. 1990. *The Decline and Fall of the British Aristocracy.* New Haven, CT: Yale University Press.

Caprio, G., and D. Klingebiel. 1997. "Bank Insolvency: Bad Luck, Bad Policy, or Bad Banking?" Annual Bank Conference on Development Economics 1996, World Bank Economic Review, January.

Chau, N., and R. Kanbur. 2001. "The Race to the Bottom, from the Bottom." Discussion Paper No. 2687: 1–51, Centre for Economic Policy Research, United Kingdom.

Chen, S., and M. Ravallion. 2001. "How Did the World's Poorest Fare in the 1990s?" Development Research Group, World Bank, Washington, D.C. Processed.

Chong, A., and M. Rama. 2001. "What Drives Public Sector Employment? Economic and Institutional Determinants across Countries." World Bank, Washington, D.C. Processed.

Claessens, S., A. Demirgüç-Kunt, and H. Huizinga. 1998. "How Does Foreign Entry Affect the Domestic Banking Market?" World Bank

Policy Research Working Paper No. 1918, World Bank, Washington, D.C.

Clark, X., D. Dollar, and A. Kraay. 2001. "Decomposing Global Inequality, 1960–99." World Bank, Washington, D.C. Processed.

Clerides, S., S. Lach, and J. Tybout. 1998. "Is 'Learning-by-Exporting' Important? Micro-Dynamic Evidence from Colombia, Mexico, and Morocco." *Quarterly Journal of Economics* 454(3): 903–47.

Coe, D., E. Helpman, and A. Hoffmaister. 1995. "North-South R&D Spillovers." National Bureau of Economic Research Working Paper No. W5048, National Bureau of Economic Research, Cambridge, MA.

Cole, M., A. Rayner, and J. Bates. 1997. "The Environmental Kuznets Curve: An Empirical Analysis." *Environment and Development Economics* 2(4): 401–16.

Collier, P. 2000. "Ethnicity, Politics, and Economic Performance." *Economics & Politics* 12(3): 225–45.

_____. 2001. "Implications of Ethnic Diversity." *Economic Policy: A European Forum* 0(**32**): 129–66.

Collier, P., and J. Dehn. 2001. "Aid, Shocks, and Growth." World Bank, Washington, D.C. Processed.

Collier, P., and D. Dollar. Forthcoming a. "Aid Allocation and Poverty Reduction." *European Economic Review.*

————. Forthcoming b. "Can the World Cut Poverty in Half?" *World Development.*

Collier, P., and J. W. Gunning. 1999. "Explaining African Economic Performance." *Journal of Economic Literature* XXXVII(March): 64–111.

Collier, P., and A. Hoeffler. 2000. "Aid, Policy, and Peace: Reducing the Risks of Civil Conflict." Development Research Group, World Bank, Washington, D.C. Processed.

_____. 2001. "Greed and Grievance in Civil War." Development Research Group, World Bank, Washington, D.C. Processed.

Collier, P., A. Hoeffler, and C. Pattillo. 2001. "Flight Capital as a Portfolio Choice." *The World Bank Economic Review* 15(1): 55–80.

Collier, P., A. Hoeffler, and M. Soderböm. 2001. "On the Duration of Civil War." Development Research Group, World Bank, Washington, D.C. Processed.

Currie, J., and A. Harrison. 1997. "Sharing the Costs: The Impact of Trade Reform on Capital and Labor in Morocco." *Journal of Labor Economics* 15(3): S44–S71.

Datt, G., and M. Ravallion. 1994. "Transfer Benefits from Public-Works Employment: Evidence for Rural India." *Economic Journal* 104(427) 1346–69.

Davis, D. R, and D. E. Weinstein. Forthcoming. "An Account of Global Factor Trade." *American Economic Review.*

Deacon, R. 1995. "Deforestation and the Rule of Law in a Cross-section of Countries." *Land Economics* 70(4): 414–30.

Dean, J. 1995. "Export Bans, Environment, and Developing Country Welfare." *Review of International Economics* 3(3): 319–29.

De Gregorio, J., S. Edwards, and R. Valdes. 1998. "Capital Controls in Chile: An Assessment." Presented at the Interamerican Seminar on Economics, Rio de Janeiro, Brazil.

Deininger, K., and L. Squire. 1996. "A New Data Set Measuring Income Inequality." *The World Bank Economic Review* 10(3): 565–91.

Demirguç-Kunt, A., R. Levine, and H. Min. 1998. "Foreign Banks: Issues of Efficiency, Fragility, and Growth." World Bank, Washington, D.C. Processed.

De Soto, H. 1989. *The Other Path: The Invisible Revolution in the Third World.* New York: Harper-Row.

Dollar, D. 1992. "Outward-Oriented Developing Countries Really Do Grow More Rapidly: Evidence from 95 LDCs, 1976–85." *Economic Development and Cultural Change* 40(3): 523–44.

_____. 2001. "Globalization, Inequality, and Poverty since 1980." World Bank, Washington, D.C. http://www.worldbank.org/research/global.

Dollar, D., and A. Kraay. 2001a. "Growth Is Good for the Poor." Policy Research Working Paper No. 2587, World Bank, Washington, D.C.

_____. 2001b. "Trade, Growth, and Poverty." Policy Research Working Paper No. 2199, World Bank, Washington, D.C.

Dollar, D., and P. Zoido-Lobatón. 2001. "Patterns of Globalization." World Bank, Washington, D.C. Processed.

Dollar, D., M. Hallward-Driemeier, T. Mengistae, O. Goswami, G. Srivastava, and A. K. Arun.

2001. "Investment Climate and Firm Productivity: India, 2000–01." World Bank, Washington, D.C. Processed.

Dowell, G., S. Hart, and B. Yeung. 2000. "Do Corporate Global Environmental Standards Create or Destroy Market Value?" *Management Science* 46(8): 1059–75.

Dunne, T., M. Roberts, and L. Samuelson. 1989. "The Growth and Failure of U.S. Manufacturing Plants." *Quarterly Journal of Economics* 104(4): 671–98.

Easterly. B., and R. Levine. 1997. "Africa's Growth Tragedy: Policies and Ethnic Divisions." *Quarterly Journal of Economics* 112(4): 1203–50.

Edmonds, E. 2001. "Will Child Labor Decline with Improvements in Living Standards?" Dartmouth College Working Paper No. 01–09, Dartmouth College, New Hampshire.

Edwards, S. 1999. "How Effective are Capital Controls?" *Journal of Economic Perspectives* 13(4): 65–84.

Encarnation, D., and L. Wells. 1986. "Evaluating Foreign Investment." In Theodore Moran, ed., *Investing in Development: New Roles for Private Capital?* 61–86, New Brunswick, NJ and Oxford: Transaction Books.

Enders, Walter, and Todd Sandler. 2000. "Is Transnational Terrorism Becoming More Threatening?" *Journal of Conflict Resolution* 44(3): 307–32.

Environics. 2001. "Poll Findings Suggest Trouble Ahead for the Globalization Agenda, Survey of 20,000 Citizens across 20 Key Countries." Available at http://www.environicsinternational.com.

Fairhead, J., and M. Leach. 1998. *Reframing Deforestation: Global Analyses and Local Realities: Studies in West Africa.* London and New York: Routledge.

Fallon, P. R., and R. Lucas. 1991. "The Impact of Changes in Job Security Regulations in India and Zimbabwe." *World Bank Economic Review* 5(3): 395–413.

FAO (Food and Agriculture Organization of the United Nations). 1999. "State of the World's Forests." Food and Agriculture Organization of the United Nations, Rome.

Feenstra, R. C., and G. H. Hanson. 1997. "Foreign Direct Investment and Relative Wages: Evidence from Mexico's Maquiladoras." *Journal of International Economics* 42(3–4): 371–93.

Finger, J. M. 1998. "GATT Experience with Safeguards: Making Economic and Political Sense of the Possibilities that the GATT Allows to Restrict Imports." Policy Research Working Paper No. 2000, World Bank, Washington D.C.

Finger, J. M., and P. Schuler. 2001. "Implementation of Uruguay Round Commitments: The Development Challenge." In B. Hoekman and W. Martin, eds., *Developing Countries and the WTO: A Pro-Active Agenda.* Oxford, Great Britain: Blackwell.

Finger, J. M., F. Ng, and W. Sonam. 2000. "Antidumping as Safeguard Policy." Paper presented to the conference on U.S.-Japan Trade Relations, Department of Economics, University of Michigan, Ann Arbor, MI.

Fink, C., A. Mattoo, and I. C. Neagu. 2001. "Trade in International Maritime Services: How Much Does Policy Matter?" Policy Research Working Paper No. 2522, World Bank, Washington, D.C.

Forteza, A., and M. Rama. 2001. "Labor Market 'Rigidity' and the Success of Economic Reforms across More than 100 Countries." Policy Research Working Paper No. 2521, World Bank, Washington, D.C.

Frankel, J. 1999. "Proposals Regarding Restrictions on Capital Flows." Harvard University. Processed.

Frankel, J., and D. Romer. 1999. "Does Trade Cause Growth?" *The American Economic Review* 89(3): 379–99.

Frankel, J., and A. Rose. 1996. "Currency Crashes in Emerging Markets: An Empirical Treatment." *Journal of International Economics* 41(3–4): 351–66.

Freeman, R., and R. Oostendorp. 2000. "Wages around the World." National Bureau of Economic Research Working Paper No. 8058, National Bureau of Economic Research, Cambridge, MA.

Freeman, R., R. Oostendorp, and M. Rama. 2001. "Globalization and Wages." World Bank, Washington, D.C. Processed.

Fretwell, D., J. Benus, and C. J. O'Leary. 1999. "Evaluating the Impact of Active Labor Market Programs: Results of Cross-country Studies in Europe and Central Asia." Social Protection Discussion Paper No. 9915, World Bank, Washington, D.C.

Fujita, M., P. Krugman, and A. J. Venables. 1999. *The Spatial Economy: Cities, Regions, and*

International Trade. : Cambridge, MA: MIT Press.

Gallego, F., L. Hernández, and K. Schmidt-Hebbel. 1999. "Capital Controls in Chile: Effective? Efficient? Endurable?" Central Bank of Chile. Processed.

Gill, I. S., F. Fluitman, and A. Dar. 2000. *Vocational Education and Training Reform: Matching Markets and Budgets.* Washington, D.C.: World Bank-Oxford University Press.

Gindling, T. H., and K. Terrell. 1995. "The Nature of Minimum Wages and Their Effectiveness as a Wage Floor in Costa Rica, 1976–91." *World Development* 23(8): 1439–58.

Government of the Netherlands. 1991. Policy Paper on Tropical Rain Forest, The Hague.

Gray, J. 1998. *False Dawn: The Delusions of Global Capitalism.* London, Great Britain: Granta Books.

Green, F., A. Dickerson, and J. S. Arbache. 2000. "A Picture of Wage Inequality and the Allocation of Labour through a Period of Trade Liberalization: The Case of Brazil." University of Kent, Canterbury, Great Britain. Processed.

Grether, J. 1996. "Mexico, 1985–1990: Trade Liberalization, Market Structure, and Manufacturing Performance." In M. Roberts and J. Tybout, eds., *Industrial Evolution in Developing Countries.* Oxford, Great Britain: Oxford University Press.

Grossman, G. 1995. "Pollution and Growth: What Do We Know?" In I. Goldin and L. Winters, eds., *The Economics of Sustainable Development.* Cambridge, England: Cambridge University Press.

Haddad, M. 1993. "The Link Between Trade Liberalization and Multi-Factor Productivity: The Case of Morocco." World Bank Discussion Paper No. 4, World Bank, Washington, D.C.

Haddad, M., and A. Harrison. 1993. "Are There Spillovers from Direct Foreign Investment? Evidence from Panel Data for Morocco." *Journal of Development Economics* 42(1): 51–74.

Haggarty, L., and M. Shirley. 2000. "Telecommunication Reform in Ghana." World Bank, Washington, D.C. Processed.

Hallward-Driemeier, M. 1997. "Understanding Foreign Direct Investment by Firms." Massachusetts Institute of Technology, Cambridge, MA. Processed.

_____. 2001. "Openness, Firms, and Competition." World Bank, Washington, D.C. http://www.worldbank.org/research/global.

Hallward-Driemeier, M., G. Iarossi, and K. Sokoloff. 2000. "Manufacturing in East Asia: Firm Level Evidence." World Bank, Washington, D.C. Processed.

Handoussa, H. 1986. "Productivity Change in Egyptian Public Sector Industries after 'the Opening,' 1973–1979." *Journal of Development Economics* 20(1): 53–73.

Harbaugh, W., A. Levinson, and D. Wilson. 2000. "Reexamining the Empirical Evidence for an Environmental Kuznets Curve." National Bureau of Economic Research Working

Paper No. 7711, National Bureau of Economic Research, Cambridge, MA.

Harrison, A. 1994. "Productivity, Imperfect Competition, and Trade Reform." *Journal of International Economics* 36(1–2): 53–73.

Hatton, T., and J. G. Williamson. 2001. "Demographic and Economic Pressure on Emigration Out of Africa." National Bureau of Economic Research Working Paper No. 8124, National Bureau of Economic Research, Cambridge, MA.

Heckman, J., and C. Pagés. 2000. "The Cost of Job Security Regulation: Evidence from Latin American Labor Markets." National Bureau of Economic Research Working Paper No. 7773, National Bureau of Economic Research, Cambridge, MA.

Henderson, V. 1996. "Effects of Air Quality Regulation." *American Economic Review* 86(4): 487–81.

Hertel, T., and W. Martin. 2001. "Liberalizing Agriculture and Manufactures in a Millennium Round: Implications for Developing Countries." In B. Hoekman and W. Martin, eds., *Developing Countries and the WTO: A Pro-Active Agenda.* Oxford, Great Britain: Blackwell.

Hoekman, B., and C. A. Primo Braga. 1997. "Protection and Trade in Services: A Survey." World Bank Working Paper No. 1747, World Bank, Washington, D.C.

Hoekman, B., H. L. Kee, and M. Olarreaga. 2001. "Markups, Entry Regulation, and Trade: Does Country Size Matter?" Policy Research Working Paper No. 2662, World Bank, Washington, D.C.

Jaffe, A., P. Peterson, P. Portney, and R. Stavins. 1995. "Environmental Regulation and the Competitiveness of U.S. Manufacturing: What Does the Evidence Tell Us?" *Journal of Economic Literature* 33(1): 132–63.

Jalan, J., and M. Ravallion. 1999. "Income Gains to the Poor from Workfare: Estimates for Argentina's Trabajar Program." Policy Research Working Paper No. 2149, World Bank, Washington, D.C.

Jaspersen, F. Z., A. H. Aylward, and A. D. Knox. 2000. "Risk and Private Investment: Africa Compared with Other Developing Areas." In P. Collier and C. Pattillo, eds., *Investment and Risk in Africa.* London and New York: MacMillan Press and St. Martin's Press.

Johnson, N. 2001. "Committing to Civil Service Reform: The Performance of Pre-Shipment Inspection Under Different Institutional Regimes." George Washington University, Washington, D.C. Processed.

Kaminsky, G., and S. Schmukler. 2001a. "Short- and Long-Run Integration: Do Capital Controls Matter?" Policy Research Working Paper No. 2660, Development Research Group, World Bank, Washington D.C.

_____. 2001b. "On Financial Booms and Crashes: Regional Patterns, Time Patterns, and Financial Liberalization." World Bank, Washington, D.C. Processed.

Kaplan, E., and D. Rodrik. 2001. "Did the Malaysian Capital Controls Work?" National Bureau of Economic Research Working Paper no. 8142, National Bureau of Economic Research, Cambridge, MA.

Kawai, M., R. Newfarmer, and S. Schmukler. 2001. "Crisis and Contagion in East Asia: Nine Lessons." World Bank Policy Research Working Paper No. 2610, World Bank, Washington, D.C.

Kokko, A. 1994. "Technology, Market Characteristics, and Spillovers." *Journal of Development Economics* 43(April): 279–93.

_____. 1996. "Local Technological Capability and Technological Spillovers from FDI in the Uruguayan Manufacturing Sector." *Journal of Development Studies* 32(April): 602–11.

Kraay, A. 1999. "Exports and Economic Performance: Evidence from a Panel of Chinese Enterprises." *Revue d' Economie du Developpement* 0(1–2): 183–207.

Kraus, C., and Z. Shalizi. 2001. "Globalization, Openness, and the Environment." World Bank, Washington, D.C. Processed.

Krugman, P. 1999. "Balance Sheets, the Transfer Problem, and Financial Crises." Massachusetts Institute of Technology, Cambridge, MA. Processed.

Lall, S., and P. Streeten. 1977. *Foreign Investment, Transnationals, and Developing Countries.* Boulder, CO: Westview Press.

Lanjouw, J. 2001. "A Patent Policy Proposal for Global Diseases." Yale University, the Brookings Institution, and the National Bureau of Economic Research. Processed.

Lanjouw, J. O., and P. Lanjouw. Forthcoming. "Rural Nonfarm Employment: An Update." *Agricultural Economics.*

Levinsohn, J. 1993. "Testing the Imports-As-Market-Discipline Hypothesis." *Journal of International Economics* 35(1/2): 1–22.

_____. 1996. "Firm Heterogeneity, Jobs, and International Trade: Evidence from Chile." National Bureau of Economic Research Working Paper No. 5808, National Bureau of Economic Research, Cambridge, MA.

Limão, N., and A. J. Venables. 2000. "Infrastructure, Geographical Disadvantage, and Transport Costs." World Bank, Washington, D.C. Processed.

Lindert, P., and J. Williamson. 2001a. "Does Globalization Make the World More Unequal?" National Bureau of Economic Research Working Paper No. 8228, National Bureau of Economic Research, Cambridge, MA.

_____. 2001b. "Globalization: A Long History." Paper prepared for the Annual Bank Conference on Development Economics-Europe conference. World Bank, Europe— Barcelona. June 25–27.

Liu, L., and J. Tybout. 1996. "Productivity Growth in Chile and Columbia: The Role of Entry, Exit, and Learning." In M. Roberts and J. Tybout, eds., *Industrial Evolution in Developing Countries.* Oxford, Great Britain: Oxford University Press.

Lumenga-Neso, O., M. Olarreaga, and M. Schiff. 2001. "On 'Indirect' Trade-Related R&D Spillovers." World Bank, Washington, D.C. Processed.

MacIsaac, D., and M. Rama. 2001. "Mandatory Severance Pay: Its Coverage and Effects in Peru." Policy Research Working Paper No. 2626, World Bank, Washington, D.C.

Maddison, A. 1995. *Monitoring the World Economy, 1820–1992.* Paris: Organisation for Economic Co-operation and Development.

_____. 2001. *The World Economy: A Millennial Perspective*. Paris: Organisation for Economic Co-operation and Development.

Maloney, W. F., and P. Fajnzylber. 2000. "Labor Demand and Trade Reform in Latin America." World Bank, Washington, D.C. Processed.

Mani, M., and D. Wheeler. 1998. "In Search of Pollution Heavens? Dirty Industry in the World Economy 1960–1995." *Journal of Environment and Development* 7(3): 215–47.

Markusen, James R. 1975. "International Externalities and Optimal Tax Structure." *Journal of International Economics* 5(1): 15–29.

Martin, W. 1997. "Measuring Welfare Changes with Distortions." In J. Francois and K. Reinert, eds., *Applied Methods for Trade Policy Analysis*. Cambridge, MA: Cambridge University Press.

_____. 2001. "Trade Policies and Developing Countries." World Bank, Washington, D.C. Processed.

Martin, W., and L. A. Winters, eds. 1996. *The Uruguay Round and the Developing Economies*. Cambridge, MA: Cambridge University Press.

McAleese, D., and D. McDonald. 1978. "Employment Growth and Development of Linkages in Foreign-owned and Domestic Manufacturing Enterprises." *Oxford Bulletin of Economics and Statistics* 40(4): 321–39.

McKinnon, R., and H. Pill. 1997. "Credible Economic Liberalizations and Over Borrowing." *American Economic Review* 87(2): 189–93.

Mishkin, F. 2001. "Financial Policies and the Prevention of Financial Crises in Emerging Market Countries." National Bureau of Economic Research Working Paper No. W8087, National Bureau of Economic Research, Cambridge, MA.

Montiel, P., and C. Reinhart. 1999. "Do Capital Controls Influence the Volume and Composition of Capital Flows? Evidence from the 1990s." *Journal of International Money and Finance* 18(4): 619–35.

Mundell, R. 2000. "A Reconsideration of the Twentieth Century." *American Economic Review* 90(3): 327–40.

Nehru, V. 1997. *China 2020: Development Challenges in the New Century*. Washington, D.C.: World Bank.

Newfarmer, R. 2001. "Multinational Corporations, Globalization, and Poverty." World Bank, Washington, D.C. Processed.

Nordstroem, H., and S. Vaughan. 1999. "Trade and Environment." World Trade Organization Special Study No. 4, World Trade Organization, Geneva, Switzerland.

Obstfeld, M. 1986. "Rational and Self-fulfilling Balance of Payments Crises." National Bureau of Economic Research Working Paper No. 1486, National Bureau of Economic Research, Cambridge, MA.

OECD (Organisation for Economic Co-operation and Development). Various years. "OECD Trends in International Migration: Continuous Reporting System on Migration." Annual report. Paris and Washington D.C.

Panday, K., and D. Wheeler. 2000. "Structural Adjustment and Forest Resources: The Impact of World Bank Operations Since 1980." World Bank Development Research Working Paper, World Bank, Washington, D.C.

Polachek, S.W. 1992. "Conflict and Trade: An Economics Approach to Political Interactions." In W. Isard and C. H. Anderson, eds., *Economics of Arms Reduction and the Peace Process.* Amsterdam, the Netherlands: North-Holland.

_____. 1997. "Why Democracies Cooperate More and Fight Less: The Relationship between International Trade and Cooperation." *Review of International Economics* 5(1): 295–309.

Rama, M. 1994. "The Labor Market and Trade Reform in Manufacturing." In M. Connolly and J. de Melo, eds., *Essays on the Effects of Protectionism on a Small Country: The Case of Uruguay.* Washington, D.C.: World Bank.

_____. 2001a. "The Gender Implications of Public Sector Downsizing: The Reform Program of Vietnam." Policy Research Working Paper No. 2573, World Bank, Washington, D.C.

_____. 2001b. "Globalization, Inequality, and Labor Market Policies." Prepared for the Annual Bank Conference on Development Economics-Europe Conference 2001, World Bank, Washington, D.C.

_____. 2001c. "The Consequences of Doubling the Minimum Wage: The Case of Indonesia." *Industrial & Labor Relations Review* 54(4): 864–81.

Ravallion, M. Forthcoming. "Growth, Inequality, and Poverty: Looking Beyond Averages." *World Development.*

Ravallion, M., and Q. Wodon. 2000. "Does Child Labor Displace Schooling? Evidence on Behavioural Responses to an Enrollment Subsidy." *The Economic Journal* 110(462): 158–75.

Ravallion, M., G. Datt, and S. Chaudhuri. 1993. "Does Maharashtra's Employment Guarantee Scheme Guarantee Employment? Effects of the 1988 Wage Increase." *Economic Development and Cultural Change* 41(2): 251–75.

Reisen, H., and H. Yeches. 1993. "Time-Varying Estimates on the Openness of the Capital Account in Korea and Taiwan." *Journal of Development Economics* 41(2): 285–305.

Revenga, A. 1997. "Employment and Wage Effects of Trade Liberalization: The Case of Mexican Manufacturing." *Journal of Labor Economics* 15(3): S20–S43.

Robbins, D. 1997. "Trade and Wages in Colombia." *Estudios de Economía* 24(1): 47–83.

Robbins, D., and T. H. Gindling. 1999. "Trade Liberalization and the Relative Wages for More-Skilled Workers in Costa Rica." *Review of Development Economics* 3(2): 140–54.

Roberts, M., and J. Tybout. 1996. *Industrial Evolution in Developing Countries: Micro Patterns of Turnover, Productivity and Market Structure.* New York: Oxford University Press.

Rodriguez, F., and D. Rodrik. 1999. "Trade Policy and Economic Growth: A Skeptic's Guide to the Cross-national Evidence." National Bureau of Economic Research, Working Paper Series No. 7081: 1–[79], April.

Rodrik, D. 1998. "Why Do More Open Economies Have Bigger Governments?" *Journal of Political Economy* 106(5): 997–1032.

Ross, M. 2001. *Timber Booms and Institutional Breakdown in Southeast Asia.* New York: Cambridge University Press.

Rudel, T., and J. Roper. 1997. "The Paths to Rain Forest Destruction: Cross-national Patterns of Tropical Deforestation, 1975–90." *World Development* 25(January): 53–65.

Sachs, J. D., A. Mellinger, and J. L. Gallup. 2001. "The Geography of Poverty and Wealth." *Scientific American* 284(3): 70–75.

Sachs, J. D., and A. Warner. 1995. "Economic Reform and the Process of Global Integration." *Brookings Papers on Economic Activity* 1(96): 1–118.

_____. 1995. "Natural Resource Abundance and Economic Growth." National Bureau of Economic Research, Working Paper Series No. 5398, National Bureau of Economic Research, Cambridge, MA.

Schmukler, S., and P. Zoido-Lobatón. 2001. "Financial Globalization: Opportunities and Challenges for Developing Countries." World Bank, Washington, D.C. Processed.

Schot, J., and K. Fischer. 1993. "The Greening of the Industrial Firm." In K. Fischer and J. Schot, eds., *Environmental Strategies for Industry.* Washington, D.C.: Island Press.

Seddon, J., and R. Wacziarg. 2001. "Trade Liberalization and Intersectoral Labor Movements." Stanford University, Stanford, CA. Processed.

Sedja, R., and R. Simpson. 1999. "Tariff Liberalization, Wood Trade Flows, and Global Forests."

Discussion Paper No. 00–05, Resources for the Future, Washington, D.C.

Sokoloff, K. 1988. "Inventive Activity in Early Industrial America: Evidence from Patent Records." *Journal of Economic History* XLVIII (4): 813–50.

Sorsa, P. 1994. "Competitiveness and Environmental Standards: Some Exploratory Results." Policy Research Paper No. 1249, International Trade Division, International Economics Department, World Bank, Washington, D.C.

Soto, C. 1997. "Controles a los Movimientos de Capitales: Evaluación Empírica del Caso Chileno." Banco Central de Chile, Santiago, Chile.

Stalker, P. 2000. *Workers without Frontiers: The Impact of Globalization on International Migration.* Geneva, Switzerland: International Labour Organization.

Sutton, J. 2000. "Rich Trade, Scarce Capabilities: Industrial Development Revisited." Discussion Paper No. EI/28 (Sept.), London School of Economics and Political Science, London, United Kingdom.

Swanson, T. 1995. "The International Regulation of Biodiversity Decline: Optimal Policy and Evolutionary Product." In C. Perrings, C. Folke, K. G. Maeler, C. Holling, and B. O. Jansson, eds., *Biodiversity Loss: Economic and Ecological Issues.* Cambridge, MA: Cambridge University Press.

Syrquin, M. 1989. "Patterns of Structural Change." In H. Chenery and T. Srinivasan, eds., *Handbook of Development Economics,* Vol. 1. Amsterdam and New York: North-Holland.

Thornton, J. 2000. *Pandora's Poison: Chlorine, Health, and a New Environmental Strategy.* Cambridge, MA: MIT Press.

Tiffen, M. 1993. "Productivity and Environmental Conservation under Rapid Population Growth: A Case Study of Machakos District." *Journal of International Development* 5(March–April): 207–23.

Tybout, J., and M.D. Westbrook. 1995. "Trade Liberalization and the Dimensions of Efficiency Change in Mexican Manufacturing Industries." *Journal of International Economics* 39(1–2): 53–78.

Ul Haque, N., N. Mark, and D. J. Mathieson. 2000. "Rating Africa: The Economic and Political Content of Risk Indicators." In P. Collier and C. Pattillo, eds., *Investment and Risk in Africa.* London and New York: MacMillan Press and St. Martin's Press.

UNCTC (United Nations Centre on Transnational Corporations). 1988. *Transnational Corporations in World Development: Trends and Prospects.* New York.

Unruh, G., and W. Moomaw. 1998. "An Alternative Analysis of Apparent EKC-Type Transitions." *Ecological Economics* 25(2): 221–29.

U.S. Immigration and Naturalization Service. 1998. *Statistical Yearbook of the U.S. Immigration and Naturalization Service,* U.S. Government Printing Office, Washington D.C., 2000.

Venables, A. J. 2001. "Geography and International Inequalities: The Impact of New Technologies." Presented at the 13th Annual Bank Conference on Development Economics, May 1–2, World Bank, Washington, D.C.

Vincent, J. 1997. "Testing for Environmental Kuznets Curves within a Developing Country." *Environment and Development Economics* 2(4): 417–31.

Von Amsberg, J. 1994. "Economic Parameters of Deforestation." Policy Research Working Paper No. 1350, World Bank, Washington, D.C.

Wacziarg, R. 1998. "Measuring the Dynamic Gains from Trade." Policy Research Working Paper No. 2001, World Bank, Washington, D.C.

Wang, H., and D. Wheeler. 1996. "Pricing Industrial Pollution in China: An Econometric Analysis of the Levy System." World Bank Policy Research Department Working Paper No. 1644, World Bank, Washington, D.C.

Wheeler, D. 2000. "Growth, Policy Management, and Environmental Institutions: Implications of the World Bank Indicator Series." World Bank Development Research Group, World Bank, Washington, D.C. Processed.

_____. 2001. "Racing to the Bottom? Foreign Investment and Air Pollution in Developing Countries." Policy Research Working Paper No. 2524, Development Research Group, World Bank, Washington, D.C.

Wheeler, D., and others. 1999. *Greening Industry: New Roles for Communities, Markets, and Governments.* New York: Oxford University Press.

Wodon, Q., and M. Minowa. 2001. "Training for the Urban Unemployed: A Reevaluation of Mexico's Probecat." In [[EDITORS]] *Proceedings of the 1999 Economists' Forum.* Washington, D.C.: World Bank.

World Bank. 1997. *Global Economic Prospects and the Developing Countries 1997.* Washington, D.C.

_____. 2000a. "Securing Our Future in a Global Economy." World Bank Latin American and Caribbean Studies, World Bank, Washington, D.C.

_____. 2000b. *Trade Blocs*. Washington, D.C.

_____. 2001a. *Finance for Growth: Policy Choices in a Volatile World*. Washington, D.C.

_____. 2001b. *Engendering Development*. Washington, D.C.

_____. 2001c. *Global Economic Prospects 2001*. Washington, D.C.

_____. 2001d. *World Development Indicators 2001*. Washington, D.C.

_____. 2001e. *World Development Report 2000/2001*. Washington, D.C.

_____. Forthcoming. *Global Economic Prospects 2002*. Washington, D.C.